The Privilege
of Persecution

The Privilege of Persecution

(And Other Things the Global Church Knows That We Don't)

Dr. Carl A. Moeller and David W. Hegg

with Craig Hodgkins

MOODY PUBLISHERS
CHICAGO

Edited by Jim Vincent
Interior design: Ragont Design
Cover design: Smartt Guys design
Cover image: Getty Images / Photodisc
Authors' Photos: C. Moeller-Len Robinson; D. Hegg-Emilee Sutherland

Library of Congress Cataloging-in-Publication Data

Moeller, Carl A.
    The privilege of persecution : and other things the global church knows that we don't / Carl Moeller and David W. Hegg ; with Craig Hodgkins.
       p. cm.
    Includes bibliographical references.
    ISBN 978-0-8024-5417-1
    1. Persecution. 2. Suffering—Religious aspects—Christianity.
    3. Pain—Religious aspects—Christianity. I. Hegg, David W.
    II. Hodgkins, Craig. III. Title.
    BR1601.3.M64 2011
    248.4—dc22
                                    2011002232

We hope you enjoy this book from Moody Publishers. Our goal is to provide high-quality, thought-provoking books and products that connect truth to your real needs and challenges. For more information on other books and products written and produced from a biblical perspective, go to www.moodypublishers.com or write to:

Moody Publishers
820 N. LaSalle Boulevard
Chicago, IL 60610
1 3 5 7 9 10 8 6 4 2

Printed in the United States of America

FROM CARL MOELLER—

To my children, Caroline, James, Claire, and Alexandra.
The greatest privilege I have is being your dad.
Thanks so much for standing with me as we
serve the persecuted. And to my amazing wife, Kim.
I thank God daily for the way in which you have given me
your love and support in this project and throughout our ministry together. You are truly a blessing beyond my dreams.

FROM DAVID W. HEGG—

To Abigail, Ellen, and Andrew.
Nothing rejoices a father's heart like watching
his children grow in their obedience to almighty God.
May your love for Christ fuel your commitment to
help keep His church reformed according to the Word.

Contents

Foreword

There is a dear brother I know—I will identify him as "S"—who lives a kind of life few of us can imagine. Hearing his story makes him seem like a character in a spy thriller. He was born a Muslim and came to faith in Christ as a young adult. That caused tremendous friction within his family. They put every imaginable pressure on him to return to Islam. When none of their efforts succeeded, they made this final offer: "We will leave you alone and stop pressuring you about your religion if . . ." The price was S's daughter—she would have to marry a fundamentalist imam. S refused the offer.

Today S travels extensively over rugged country, meeting with followers of Jesus, all of whom have come out of Islam. These believers meet in small house fellowships, varying the time and location to avoid detection by neighbors. In this area dominated by a radical sect of Islam, hundreds have discovered the truth of the gospel. S brings them books and recordings to help them grow in their faith. He encourages the leaders of these house churches. And he lifts the spirits of all the believers with his smile, strong hugs, and passionate prayers.

Recently as S was moving between villages he was ambushed by a group of militants who demanded that he convert back to Islam or they would kill him. Miraculously he escaped, but he was shot in the leg and for many weeks was unable to return to his ministry. When a friend of mine recently met him in a secret location they could talk for only an hour. S was excited about a new project that would teach the Scriptures through music for the many in his area who are illiterate. When asked how we could pray, he answered: "The believers are too scattered. Pray that there will be more opportunity for us to experience community." He also expressed concern for the children of the believers. They are asking hard questions of their parents such as "Why do you believe a different religion than everyone else?"

Through S I have a glimpse of daily life of believers living under persecution. It's an incredible challenge to live out one's faith in the midst of such hostility. But S demonstrates for me the victorious faith so many of our brothers and sisters experience despite all of the opposition. Their faith passes the most severe tests and reveals God's power. These believers know God intimately and have the kind of faith that I want.

If this is the kind of radical faith you want to experience, then you are holding the right book in your hands. Carl and David have studied the global church, much of it living under restriction and persecution, and they have discovered what it will take to bring new life to you and your church.

I was a young man on my first missionary journey to Poland when God spoke to me from His Word: "Wake up! Strengthen what remains and is about to die" (Revelation 3:2 NIV). That was my calling to go and strengthen the church under persecution, and it has been the work of Open Doors since 1955. But today I hear that plea from our Lord for the church in America and throughout the free world. We need the vitality of faith displayed by those living in what we often call the third world.

In recent years as I've traveled in the West, people have said to me, "Brother Andrew, what the church needs is a revival. We are praying for revival." I disagree! What the church needs is reformation! Revival will put more people in the pews. Reformation will transform the thinking and behavior of the church and reveal Jesus to a broken world. *That* is what we need.

The church under persecution experiences worship and prayer to a depth few of us have experienced. However, we can have that intimacy with God; they can show us how. Further, these fellow believers have learned to live in community among a hostile culture. They may never be able to influence their culture but that doesn't change their commitment to live out their faith and to share that faith with the lost. Perhaps most surprising, churches with nothing can teach us who have so much what sacrificial giving looks like. I have experienced some of the most incredible hospitality from people who have nothing yet share everything they do have.

Carl and David explore six areas where the global church can teach us what reformation looks like. So I hope your hearts are ready to be challenged. You and I are part of a worldwide body of Christ. Parts of that body are suffering, even struggling for their very survival. They have learned about vital faith through fire. We need them. We need to hear what they have learned. We need to listen to the voice of God speaking through them, for they have much to give to us.

That's why I believe when you are finished reading this book you will agree with me that in our churches it can no longer be "business as usual." No, it's time for the church in the free world to awaken and be all that God wants her to be.

—BROTHER ANDREW, Founder, Open Doors

Opening Words about the Global Church

Many Americans view the global church as "third-world," needy, uneducated, and poor—sorely lacking in much of what we assume the church needs to function well. But the irony is that we're in much greater need of them.

It is a lesson that is best viewed through a lens of humility, and both of us have had to learn in our own way.

* * *

When I first joined Open Doors USA as president and CEO, I was struck by the subtle paternalism that we in the West have toward our fellow believers around the globe. I realized that so many of our assumptions and perspectives about them are absolutely false. The global church is at once both more simple and more complex than we in the West tend to realize. In short, they are more like us than we realize.

In America, pastors are so accustomed to looking to the megachurch down the street or across the country for innovations that they can "import" to their churches to make them more vibrant, relevant, and successful. I know, because I have served as a pastor at more than one large Western church. But after traveling to multiple countries on every continent, I have experienced firsthand the Christlike approach these believers have toward every aspect of their lives. I have come to believe that their vibrant, sacrificial, and communal faith is often much closer to God's intent for His church and His children.

Another stereotype we frequently have is that the global church is all the same. But God's church varies not only from country to country, but also from region to region within countries. For example, some countries have established traditional churches and others operate through the house church movement. In addition, the persecution that believers face around the globe can differ widely. In some regions, it originates from majority religions; in others, directly from the government. Sometimes persecution results in social injustice or a loss of personal freedoms. Sometimes it results in injury and death.

There's definitely a place for understanding persecution in the West. If Scripture says all believers who desire to live a godly life will be persecuted (see 2 Timothy 3:12), what does that look like to us? The concept of persecution comes with a certain acknowledgment that there's going to be a struggle. What is our struggle? How well are we doing with it? These are just a few of the important questions David and I want to ask in this book.

—CARL MOELLER

Over the years my association with Open Doors USA has taken me down a road I didn't even know existed. At first, I approached the cause of the persecuted church as most Western believers do, from the point of view of our strength and their weakness. They were poor, and needy, and largely undertrained and underresourced. They greatly needed us, and we felt so good about ourselves when we rode in on our Western ideas and resources to rescue them. That's what I thought until I got on a plane and flew to meet them, in their homes, on their soil, in their churches. It didn't take long to recognize that they had a deep and humble dependence on Christ that fueled a faith that was extraordinary.

Their priorities were what I wanted mine to be, and their love and mutual care were already what I was constantly exhorting our congregation to become. It turns out they needed our resources, but we greatly needed their depth of insight into everyday dependence upon Christ and His church. Writing this book with Carl offered me the chance to share what I have learned with Christ-followers who can benefit greatly through observing the lives and wisdom of those who share our faith but not our freedom. We who are free need to understand the privilege of persecution, used in the hands of the Savior, to align our priorities and focus our ministry on the things that will matter for eternity.

—DAVID W. HEGG

Pain makes man think.
Thought makes man wise.
Wisdom makes life endurable.

JOHN PATRICK
The Teahouse of the August Moon, act 1, scene 1

He is not truly patient who will
suffer only as much as he pleases,
or from whom he pleases.

THOMAS À KEMPIS
The Imitation of Christ

Introduction

L ike many employees in the early days of the Walt Disney Studios, Albert Hurter was an extremely gifted artist. Hand-drawn animation was and is a labor-intensive medium, with sharply defined responsibilities carried out in near-assembly-line fashion by hundreds of talented artists wielding pencils, pens, and paint. And it wasn't a quick process. Each animated feature required an average of three years to complete, from the initial storyboards, audio recordings, and pencil animation to the inking of cels, painting of backgrounds, and the filming—one frame at a time—of the final composited color elements.

Hurter's role on the staff was as unique as his personality. Nearly fifty years old when he joined Disney in 1931—his fellow employees were mainly in their twenties at the time, and Walt himself was only twenty-nine—he was a native of Switzerland, and was so methodical and punctual that studio employees set their watches by his comings and goings. But unlike the rest of the staff, he was not a story man, an animator, a pen-and-inker, or a background painter.

He was the Disney Studio's very first inspirational sketch artist.

Each day, Hurter would create hundreds of illustrations to stimulate the imaginations of the studio's story men and animators; drawings of fanciful creatures, mood studies, and group scenes; or intricate structural details and building interiors. He is credited with inspiring the look and feel of many cartoon shorts, and he made substantial contributions to Disney's first two animated features, *Snow White and the Seven Dwarfs* and *Pinocchio*. And, despite his austere and introverted nature, he was the man everyone came to for artistic help and advice, a common occurrence that lead to one brief but telling exchange that lives on in Disney Studio lore. One day a young artist "asked Hurter to critique a much-labored-over perspective drawing: 'Don't spare my feelings. Just tell me if there's anything wrong with this,' said the youngster, to which Hurter solemnly remarked, 'Nothing is right with this.'"[1]

It is not our intent to render an Albert Hurter–like verdict on the American church. Indeed, there is much that is "right" with it. There are countless examples of courageous, socially engaged, God-fearing people who are doing the work of Christ in communities across the nation. And yet we also recognize that in some dimensions of our spiritual life—and in some churches and denominations—we aren't doing as well as we could be.

But we don't have to get it all wrong to admit that we need to get better.

At the same time, we want to avoid "hyperspiritualizing" the global church, or as we will more often call it in this book, the persecuted church. The persecuted church is not made up of flawless believers. Like the church in the West, it is composed of human believers who sin and struggle with their own personal and cultural baggage.

It's just that our bags don't look alike.

And so, with this book, we seek to accomplish what Hurter did during the majority of his working hours: provide a variety of illustrations designed to instruct and inspire. And these illustrations will be personal experiences and examples of daily disciplines from the persecuted church.

What Is the Persecuted Church?

But before we can learn anything from these courageous examples, we must first establish just who, or what, the persecuted church is.

First, the persecuted church includes many if not most believers outside the West. Much has been written in recent years about the growth of the global church—the rise of Christianity in Africa, Asia, and Latin America. What has not always been mentioned, though it should be, is that many believers in the global South live under threat of persecution. Indeed, the global church and the persecuted church are, in large part, one and the same.

Second, the intentional persecution of God's people manifests itself differently around the globe. It most commonly takes place in countries or regions where Christ-followers are in the minority, and where other religions have traditionally dominated the culture. Sometimes the persecution comes at the hands of the government itself, and sometimes from the leaders of the majority faiths.

For some believers, persecution means the denial of civil rights; to others, it means being ostracized socially or abandoned by their families. And tragically, for many, it results in serious injury and death. But persecution is not static. Each year, the situations improve in some countries, and grow worse in others.

But persecution, pressure, and pain seem to bring about differing results, depending on where they occur. In America, pressure and pain seem to drive people away from God. But in the global church outside North America, it tends to drive people toward Him, and there is often a genuine sense of honor that they get a chance to suffer for Jesus Christ.

Pain as a Privilege

The persecuted church sees pain as a privilege.

How can that be? That question is one of the many issues we will explore here. But here is a short answer.

In the West, the deceitfulness of riches and the confidence of comfort can lead to spiritual dullness, which prevents us from knowing where the edge of danger really is, and we can fall right over the edge into the abyss. In the persecuted church—because of the constant threats and opposition of the enemy—believers stay crystal clear as to where the edge is; they understand that every aspect of their commitment to Christ is a battleground. We've become accustomed to tolerating sin and deceitful things in our lives, so much so that we often no longer recognize them as sin and deceit.

Every human endeavor, when repeated over time, runs the risk of succumbing to an inevitable dulling effect, which means that the same can be true of prayer, worship, and generosity. These and other spiritual weapons—and our senses—can become rusty due to overexposure to the elements and lack of care. But the persecuted live in an abrasive environment. They are never allowed to get too comfortable. Their weapons of worship and prayer remain sharp through constant use and a supportive community, where iron sharpens iron. And, since they're constantly being rubbed by the steel wool of their culture, the rust doesn't ever have time to accumulate.

If every time a believer shares his faith he could potentially be turned in to the authorities—by the person he's witnessing to—and thrown in prison, then the simple act of sharing his faith becomes a faith decision of its own. Each time will be real and meaningful. If every time a pastor or teacher shares the Word of God he runs the risk of arrest, or attack, or the threat of harm to his family and loved ones, then teaching God's Word becomes a real, palpable faith decision as well. And each time we choose to obey God's call on our lives, we get a little bit sharper, a little less rusty.

Due to the constant honing and sharpening they experience, there really is no sense of discontent within the persecuted church for these simple disciplines of the faith, either among pastors or the believers themselves. Some of these pastors have been serving their communities for twenty or thirty years. Many have had to remain underground, some have been in prison, but there is no discontent.

Because they constantly face new challenges, or the same difficult challenges over and over, they have learned that God's great faithfulness can be new every morning.

In the West, we struggle to understand how fellow believers in other countries can maintain their faith in the midst of such difficult trials, and indeed why they choose to do it. But there's really only one explanation: The Spirit of God has come into their lives and revealed the truth to them. They regard that truth as a pearl of such great price that they would sell everything they have in order to get it.

Perhaps we have become so enthralled—and weighted down —by the many strands of cultured pearls wrapped around our necks that we've lost the ability to recognize a real pearl when we see one.

As odd as it may sound, pastors and believers in the persecuted church have a great deal of compassion for those of us in the West. They often pray that all of our wealth and all of our distractions won't draw us away from our faith, from our first love of Jesus, or from the mission God has entrusted us with. It can be difficult for someone who has been fully immersed in the culture of the persecuted church to relate to Western believers who think it's a really tough day when their daughter doesn't make the cheerleading squad. And yet, those in the persecuted church understand that they can't blame somebody for not having had a more difficult existence. We must grow where we are planted.

They understand that the body of Christ is one body, and that the Enemy uses a large variety of individualized schemes to undermine and divide us. Satan never tests the Western church and the persecuted church using the same form of temptation, but the function of those individualized temptations is always the same: to separate and disempower us.

But the blessings God brings in these times of trial are personalized as well.

For example, to us, a promotion at work may seem like a blessing, but the Enemy will try to use it to bring added greed and temptation as well as reduced family time. Conversely, a jail sentence may seem like a curse to someone in a persecuted culture, but God may use it to bring the blessing of time to renew a tired faith.

The truth is that there is much more commonality to be found in our experiences than the superficial assessment of what our relative statuses in this life may lead us to believe.

When we read the parables of Jesus with fresh eyes, we see that there is never a promise of material benefit to following Jesus. Believers in the persecuted church know that truth from personal experience, and yet millions every year turn to faith in Christ in countries where it's hardest to convert, places where there are no social or economic or political benefits to being a believer. In countries such as Pakistan and Afghanistan, the only reason people would take such a huge personal faith step is because God has revealed the truth to them, and the truth has set them free.

But perhaps because we've grown up in a culture inspired by Judeo-Christian values, and are largely surrounded by people with an appreciation for them—even if they don't believe in God or the Christian message—we have forgotten how radically different God's truth really is from the worldly culture, and how different we are called to be.

Instead, we often find ourselves looking for a rational pathway to radical discipleship, but that path may be hard to find in our culture, even with a strong rational faith.

Just like Solomon's Problem

In the West, we have the problem of Solomon.

Solomon inherited a magnificent heritage of righteousness

from his father, David. He had tremendous privilege and absolute power, and in many ways he started off well. He asked God for wisdom, and received it. But when we look a little deeper, we realize that Solomon's experience was different from that of the previous rulers. Saul had squandered a kingdom, David earned a kingdom, but Solomon inherited a kingdom.

Solomon had no reason to feel guilty about inheriting his father's kingdom. God didn't blame Solomon for being rich. Likewise, Americans shouldn't feel guilty about being one of the wealthiest nations on earth. Extreme wealth can be a significant barrier to some things, but it's also important to internalize and come to terms with it.

But here's where Solomon's experience really parallels our own: When Solomon began his journey, he understood humility before the Lord. The challenges came later.

As he began to be more and more comfortable in the luxuries he was given, and in everything else he had acquired, he began to slowly push the boundaries of what was appropriate and acceptable in God's eyes. He almost certainly continued to go to the temple all the time—he had built it, after all—but he eventually acquired more than a thousand wives and concubines, and then made accommodation for idolatry within his own home. He provided a platform for the worship of multiple gods within the heart of the Jewish nation; he brought the very enemies of God to the seat of his kingdom. And, although we don't have much information in Scripture about it, odds are that he also had advisors from all of these countries of the wives he married, and that he supported the priests of Baal and Dagon with the tithes of the people of Israel.

Solomon was able to maintain his own personal relationship to the living God for many years, but all of the other things ultimately destroyed him. And he knew it. Just read the book of Ecclesiastes:

"Meaningless! Meaningless!" says the Teacher. "Utterly meaningless! Everything is meaningless." What does man gain from
all his labor at which he toils under the sun? Generations
come and generations go, but the earth remains forever.
(Ecclesiastes 1:2–4 NIV)

In spite of the riches, fame, women, power . . . even the
wisdom . . . at the end of his days, Solomon could only say, "Everything is meaningless."

Like Solomon, the American church has been blessed with an
inheritance. The founders of our country asked God for wisdom,
and then crafted the many freedoms we've been able to enjoy for
more than two hundred years, including the freedom to worship
God openly and without persecution. But as we became accustomed to our wealth, we have brought the values of the Enemy
into our courtyards, and now—even in our churches—we often
can't distinguish the truth from a lie.

In all honesty, it was easier for our forefathers to envision a life
of sacrifice followed by eternal rewards than it is for us. We've
become unaccustomed to deferred hope. Our culture of imme-
diate gratification has convinced us that whatever we can get here
and now is far better than what we'd ever potentially receive in the
future. *It's a win-win situation!* we tell ourselves.

At the end of Solomon's reign, his legacy was not one of knowledge and wise, skilled living. He had squandered his godly inheritance, and the kingdom he passed on to his son was in complete
disarray. It fractured early on, revealing that there was nothing at
the core. Faith in God had almost become extinct in vast portions
of the kingdom.

The question for the American church is no different. What are
we doing with our godly inheritance? What sort of faith are we
modeling for—and leaving to—our children, and to their children?

A Lesson from the Lowly Artichoke

As citizens of the United States, we don't often look at it in this context, but the majority of our forefathers were persecuted Christians. They all came—the Puritans, the Pilgrims, the Catholics, the Quakers, and others—out of a sense of desperation, to find a place where they could practice their faith.

And yet, despite our humble beginnings, we often completely misunderstand and underestimate the persecuted church. When we look at it through our Western mind-set, we see it as under-resourced, undereducated, and therefore deficient.

But the persecuted church is like an artichoke.

The outside of an artichoke is not very appealing, certainly not as eye-catching as the streamlined cucumber or the vibrantly colored tomato. In fact, it is hard to imagine how anybody could have ever expected it to be edible. But thankfully, someone did. As you begin to eat it, you find that in spite of their toughness, the outside leaves do have some flavor, and provide some nutritional value. But the artichoke is all about delayed gratification. The real benefit comes as you get further inside, because the further in you go, the better it gets. The leaves grow more tender, more flavorful. And when you get to the heart—the slightly sweet, meaty center—that's the best thing of all.

We've allowed ourselves—and our churches—to accumulate a vast number of outer leaves. But as these things have attached themselves to our hearts, they have become an aggregate wall around the good, sweet meat of the gospel.

So we need to do what the persecuted church does. We need to worry less about the appearance and texture of our outside leaves—the things we "layer on" because we think they make our churches better—and focus on the heart of things. And examining the attitudes and the practices of those in the persecuted church is a great way to do that. Their church life is way less convenient.

They sometimes have to walk two and a half miles to church. They don't have enough food or medical care. Many of their governments won't even let them meet together. Some of them go to prison. But are they better off spiritually?

In all honesty, much of the time they are.

The church in the developing and persecuted world has much to teach us simply because they still understand—and still remember—what it felt like to hear and receive the gospel.

And that's what we need to get back to.

So we must adopt again the motto of the Christian reformers, which is *"Ecclesia reformata, semper reformanda secundum verbum Dei,"* or, for those of us who don't read Latin, "The church reformed, always being reformed according to the Word of God."

Time for an After-Action Review

In times of war or peace, military leaders are expected to write up daily reports known as AARs, or After-Action Reviews. These reviews provide soldiers and units with feedback on mission and task performances in training and in combat. They are practical: AARs identify how to correct deficiencies, sustain strengths, and focus on performance of specific mission-essential tasks such as training objectives.

The real key to the success of an AAR is an open climate. The soldiers and leaders honestly discuss what actually transpired in sufficient detail and clarity so that everyone can understand what did and did not occur and why and, most importantly, everyone will have a strong desire to seek the opportunity to practice the task again.

Because they are filed daily, the plans are constantly updated as new and better information comes to light. Pride and stubbornness can't be allowed to factor into the mix, because—especially in time of war—any false assumption or mistake that is made can cause severe consequences. People can die. The goal of the AAR is simply to improve, to enable everyone to be better equipped to carry out the mission at hand. Competent leaders want to understand and apply what the AARs teach them.[2]

So consider this book to be an After-Action Review filed on behalf of the persecuted church for the betterment of their brothers in arms in the West. In these pages, we'll examine six major areas where the church in the West has a good deal to learn from those in the persecuted church.

Although there will be some overlap from chapter to chapter and topic to topic, these primary areas of focus are:

- God and His Word
- Worship and the Church
- Prayer and Dependence
- Community, Culture, and Evangelism
- Leadership, Authority, and Power
- Generosity and Stewardship

We pray that, in the spirit of God—and perhaps even in the memory of Albert Hurter—you will be inspired to imagine what a renewed faith can bring about in your personal lives, and in the life of churches everywhere. We pray that the courage and daily practices of those in the persecuted church will cause you to examine what you believe, the way you think, and the way you choose to act on those thoughts and beliefs.

To God be the glory.

All Scripture is inspired by God and profitable for teaching, for reproof, for correction, for training in righteousness; so that the man of God may be adequate, equipped for every good work.

2 TIMOTHY 3:16–17

So will My word be which goes forth from My mouth; it will not return to Me empty, without accomplishing what I desire, and without succeeding in the matter for which I sent it.

ISAIAH 55:11

1

God and His Word

Once while visiting the United States, a group of believers from the persecuted church in North Korea spent some time with a pastor's family in the Pacific Northwest. On Sunday they attended church in the morning, and then joined Pastor Hogan (not his real name) and another group for lunch, while his family returned home. When the North Korean visitors arrived back at the pastor's house, his teenaged son was sitting on the couch reading his Bible. When the guests entered the room, he rose to be polite. As he did, he reached back and lightly tossed his Bible on the cushions behind him.

The visitors began to weep.

Pastor Hogan was at a loss, and anxiously asked his guests what was wrong. They answered his question with one of their own. "How can he treat the Word of God in such a manner?"

To many of us in the West, the emotional reverence of these men for a book, even a very special book, may seem too dramatic, but there is an irresistible sense of grandeur that comes when the Bible is viewed as something possessing the awe and the nobility of God Himself. The Bible is no mere historical document. True, it is a written record of God's dealings with men and His revelation of Himself and His will, and it is the bestselling book of all time.

But it is so much more.

"For the word of God is living and active and sharper than any two-edged sword, and piercing as far as the division of soul and spirit, of both joints and marrow, and able to judge the thoughts and intentions of the heart" (Hebrews 4:12).

The Book or *A* Book?

Throughout history, millions have been put to death because they refused to deny the infallible truth revealed in line after line within its covers. And today, in oppressive nations around the globe, believers continue to be persecuted for their faith. Many choose to die rather than turn their back on God's Word.

And the visitors from North Korea aren't alone in their perspective. In Egypt and Pakistan, in Iran and Cambodia, persecuted believers see God's Word as God's *word*, and they treat it with great reverence. They acknowledge its authority, and that the authority comes from Him. They know that God speaks to us today through His Word, and that the Word of God is the written word.

That's a perspective that we often miss.

Here, we're able to build churches and bring people to God with our methods, our techniques, our knowledge, and our technology, but we are nowhere near as humble before God as those who do not have all of those things, who simply and faithfully revere His Holy Word.

Few third-world pastors have ever received any formal training or resources. Most carry just one book with them. But that book is a Bible, often with hundreds of handwritten notes scribbled in the margins, the insights from lessons they have given and received throughout their years of ministry. They hold God's Word in the highest regard, and are hesitant to part with it. In fact, it is not unusual for one of these pastors to continue carrying his Bible in a small, lidded box long after the original book covers become too worn to protect the treasure contained within.

That sort of individualized care for a single book rarely occurs here, because our well-stocked libraries are not only full of books, they are stacked high with Bibles in a variety of translations, interpretations, annotations, bindings, and printings. We have study Bibles, reference Bibles, parallel Bibles, amplified Bibles, red-letter Bibles, and life-application Bibles. We have Bibles for men, for women, for teens, and for children; for soldiers, motorcyclists, grandmothers, and patriots.

In true Western fashion, some of these special editions feature a pastor or scholar's name on the cover, sometimes in a font larger than the words *Holy Bible*, because recognizable brand names sell more books. In the four centuries since the King James Version of the Bible was first published, those names above the title have gone from Thompson, Scofield, Harper, and Holman to a long list of today's most popular teachers and preachers. Although these works often offer valuable scholarship and specialized study aids, they can make it appear as if the Bible has become a movie starring a well-known pastor or scholar and costarring God Himself.

So it should come as no surprise that, at least in the West, the Bible is in danger of being viewed, and treated, as *a* book rather than *the* book.

Reverence for the Father's Book

Brother Andrew, the dynamic founder of Open Doors, always refers to the Bible as "Father's book." Every time he speaks with anyone—especially in the Islamic world, where he now spends so much of his ministry time—he refers to it in that manner. His reasoning is sound, for when God is encountered as father and not as a judge, it presumes a relationship with the Almighty that the Muslim world doesn't understand, and the natural curiosity that results often creates an honest dialogue.

Because of how they treat their sacred Quran, Muslims already understand the concept of reverence for a book. In 2009, Andrew visited a radical madrassa—an Islamic seminary—in the Middle East to preach the good news of Jesus Christ. Lifting his Bible up for all to see, he told the students there, "I show thee Father's book. This is the book that teaches how Jesus died for you."

When he was finished speaking, he presented a special copy of the New Testament to the imam in charge of the seminary, who took the Word of God and reverently kissed it before placing it respectfully on a stand, just as he would have done for the Quran.

For many Christians in America, such respect for God's Word is rare. Although the average believer may have up to half a dozen Bibles in their home, they seldom carry one with them and do not read it regularly.

The Word surrounds us, but that doesn't mean it automatically sinks in. You can lead a Christian to God's Word, but you can't make him drink deeply of it.

Perhaps, as A. W. Tozer wrote forty years ago, we have lost our grip on the "high view" of God and His Word:

> The Church has surrendered her once lofty concept of God and has substituted for it one so low, so ignoble, as to be utterly unworthy of thinking, worshiping men. . . . With our loss of the sense of majesty has come the further loss of religious awe and consciousness of the divine Presence. . . . This loss of the concept of majesty has come just when the forces of religion are making dramatic gains and the churches are more prosperous than at any time within the past several hundred years. But the alarming thing is that our gains are mostly external and our losses wholly internal; and since it is the *quality* of our religion that is affected by internal condi-

tions, it may be that our supposed gains are but losses spread over a wider field.[1]

Today, we can choose from more than thirty English translations of the Bible. For nearly three centuries in the English-speaking world, the King James Bible was all anyone had. Although there has never been a shortage of opinions about Bible scholarship, it is generally agreed that the KJV is not a perfect translation. It contains sections that aren't found in any manuscript, and the book of Revelation had to be translated from the Latin to the Greek to English. But did God use the King James Bible to speak to generation after generation of His children? Absolutely.

He also used a donkey to get His message across to the reluctant prophet Balaam. With God, it's not about the messenger; it's about the message.

Clarity through God's Word

God has always sought to bring clarity out of confusion and light out of shadow in order to illuminate our lives, and He has chosen to accomplish this through His written Word. As J. I. Packer has noted in his classic, *Knowing God*:

He made us with the intention that He and we may walk together forever in a love relationship. But such a relationship can only exist when the parties involved know something of each other. God, our Maker, knows all about us before we say anything (Psalm 139:1–4); but we can know nothing about Him unless He tells us. Here, therefore, is a further reason why God speaks to us: not only to move us to do what He wants, but to enable us to know Him so that we may love Him. Therefore God sends His word to us in the character of both information and invitation. It comes to woo us as well as to instruct us; it not merely puts us in the picture of what God has done and is doing, but also calls us into personal communion with the Lord Himself.[2]

In the first century, God's Word brought the early church out of darkness and into the dazzling light of relationship with Him. Today, even in areas of the most intense persecution, new believers are experiencing the same thing. They are coming out of Hinduism, out of Buddhism, and out of Islam, so they recognize darkness. And using the testimony of "secret believers" in the global church, and through His Spirit, God meets them where they are. Because of these experiences, they can sense, even without teaching or training, that this God—the one true God, the God of Abraham, Isaac, and Jacob—can bring light.

So when they finally come face-to-face with the Bible, and are able to read it for the first time with their own eyes, the Scriptures have an undeniable ring of truth. Because of what these new Christians have learned from fellow believers who have risked their lives to share their faith, what these new followers read is consistent with what they know to be true about God and His Holy Word. In a sense, now that they possess the written Word of God, passed down through generations of believers, it becomes a filter through which all of their previous experiences must pass. In a land of spiritual darkness, where people have visions of all kinds, they must learn to recognize what is of God, and what is not, and the Bible becomes a self-authenticating witness to them.

The Modern Mind and the Relevant Word of God

But this self-authenticating power of God's Word is often overlooked today in the West. For instead of recognizing its power, we come to it with our analytical minds; that critical and cynical mind-set that prefers to dissect things and attempt to break them down to their most basic elements. We don't take to sacred things very easily or comfortably, and our culture at large certainly doesn't trust anything that seeks to place itself higher up on the postmodern food chain. The natural first inclination of modern man is to attempt to undermine everything, to stick a pin in to see if it pops.

Yet even as the critics among us try their best to pick it apart, they also insist that they can bring something of equal value to it, something to improve upon it, and that something is "relevance."

IF THE BIBLE IS the Word of the
eternal God . . . then it is eternally relevant.

But if the Bible is the Word of the eternal God, which the testimonies of both God and Jesus say it is, then it is eternally relevant. Instead, what we in the church must do is communicate it in a manner that is understandable to our culture, an intentional process vastly different from adapting the message to conform to our culture. To do anything else to God's Word is the height of impiety. Packer declares:

> The claim of the word of God upon us is absolute: the word is to be received, trusted, and obeyed, because it is the word of God the king. The essence of impiety is the proud willfulness of "this evil people, which refuse to hear my words" (Jeremiah 13:10). The mark of true humility and godliness, on the other hand, is that a man "trembleth at my word" (Isaiah 66:2).[3]

But when we come to the Word of God, we often do so with the same approach we may take with Christianity in general, which means it is often treated like just another "self-help" book, something we may flip through to discover a few tips, tricks, or secrets to make our family, friends, and work life a more personally satisfying experience.

But the Bible could not be any less like a self-help book. It is, in fact, a completely alien book. It speaks of a God who is holy and wholly different than the gods of our culture, and from the gods of any other culture down through human history. We must approach it in the same way a former Muslim did when he recently received his first opportunity to read from the pages of God's Holy Word.

His incredulous reaction was, "I cannot believe that I now have the keys in my hand for this personal experience with God. I can find Him in here, and in here He will speak truth."

His whole world had been turned upside down, as it had for the scores of Muslim converts who came before him. These converts will leave their families if they have to, as many are forced to do so; they will leave their culture, as they are now aliens themselves, because they have chosen to follow the God whose Word is completely alien to their culture.

But that's not the road we in the West want to travel. We don't always want to hear or read the truth. We simply want the Bible to help make us better people within our culture.

Not a *Better* Person—a *Different* Person

We cannot expect God's Word to make each of us into a "better" person. It does, however, have the power to make each of us into a completely different person: the person whom God intended us originally to be, a person created in the image of Christ.

The Westminster Assembly completed the Westminster Shorter Catechism in 1647. Comprising 107 questions with corresponding answers and biblical proof texts, the catechism was intended for use by Christian families and churches. The questions and answers are brief and to the point, including this brisk exchange for question #2:

Q: *What rule hath God given to direct us how we may glorify and enjoy Him?*
A: The Word of God, which is contained in the Scriptures of the Old and New Testaments, is the only rule to direct us how we may glorify and enjoy Him.

Pastors and teachers from the global church understand this distinction. They approach the Bible as a living and active and powerful Word (Hebrews 4:12). They know that it is the primary way for us to hear the voice of God today, and that it is not like any other work of literature.

But we tend to take a different approach. Maybe we're not as respectful of it as we should be. It is doubtful if any modern pastors worry about having to duck behind the pulpit if they say something that isn't true of God. But is there any fear in our hearts that we should have studied harder? Are we engaging with God's Word enough—and in the right spirit of humility—to prepare ourselves for the honor and privilege of teaching God's people each weekend?

Instead of approaching God's Word with the holy awe it deserves, some pastors and teachers treat the Bible as just another ingredient in their weekend omelet recipe. And because modern church congregations have all sorts of different tastes, they throw a wide variety of other ingredients into the mixing bowl as well. And, if people seem to enjoy the omelet after it is served, then the pastor and his team consider themselves successful for another week.

A Craving for Experience
Instead of Knowledge

We seem to have replaced our healthy thirst for knowledge with a passion for experience. Both are lofty objectives and admirable traits, but like the rest of our lives, they should be kept in balance. Thomas Boston, the seventeenth-century British pastor, said, "Knowledge is a necessary foundation of faith and holiness; and where ignorance reigns in the mind, there is confusion in the heart and life." For years, this was a given in pulpits throughout the United States. But although knowledge dominated organized religion for centuries, experience and personal comfort have usurped it more recently.

Thirty-five years ago, one of the top sellers was J. I. Packer's *Knowing God*. A couple of decades later, Henry Blackaby's *Experiencing God* topped the sales charts. Both books are excellent and remain extremely relevant, yet the Blackaby title reveals the current focus on feelings and experience. It's one more example that—in the span of twenty-five years—Western believers have shifted their passions from knowledge to experience.

Today, a pastor who wants to start a large church in America may find his biggest expenditure besides the building to be the sound system in the worship center, because music is where most people find a connection in our culture of experience and entertainment. A video screen also would play a key role. That order of priorities often plays out in the way God's Word is used in the service. Most of our sermons begin with compelling stories pulled from current events, and are frequently topical, "one-off" messages instead of being part of a series, because many people don't attend every week. And because messages are often topical, a pastor will probably "parachute" into the text, meaning that he will pull a verse or verses out of their structural context in order to support his topical point.

Making the Scriptures Central

Parachuting into text is acceptable in small doses, for sometimes it is the only way to quickly get to an important parallel truth in the midst of another message. But when it occurs frequently over time, people can begin to view the Bible as a sort of spiritual encyclopedia or God's "Big Rule Book." This lack of understanding leads to questions such as, "Where does the Bible say we should do this?" or "Where does it say we shouldn't do that?"

Ironically, these types of questions don't often arise out of theological discussions. Instead, they most often crop up when one person is trying to win an argument with another person about a social issue or a political position, but they prefer to have an answer that sounds more spiritual.

It is questions such as these that lead people to search the Scriptures in vain for one of the most famous non-verses of all, "The Lord helps those who help themselves."

This shift away from the centrality of God's Word in weekend messages is a significant issue, for Satan can attack a church through the use of a common vernacular that becomes so diluted with examples from our general culture that it runs the risk of becoming indistinguishable from our general culture.

This doesn't mean that pastors should speak without using stories, illustrations, or visual support. On the contrary, pastors should use everything at their disposal so that they may preach in a manner that causes their congregations to better understand God's Word. We don't need more pastors who need to pass out secret decoder rings so their people can understand what he is saying.

Each message should originate from God's Word and flow outward, rather than the other way around.

Of course, while they should be committed to making the message simple to understand, pastors must take care to not make it simplistic, which is not the same thing.

While God *does* require a child-*like* faith, He does not approve of a child-*ish* conviction. Coming into fellowship with God is a simple act of responding to God's mercy and love. But comprehending His truth, and experiencing a lifetime of fruitfulness, takes sheer discipline—a lot of hard work. The study of the things of God requires a rigorous use of our minds.[4]

Pastors in the global church frequently ask open-ended questions such as, "What's the story of the Bible?" or "What was God thinking when He gave us the Bible over a 1,600-year period?" They trust the Bible, so they work hard to understand the context of it. They want to go deeper and wider.

If they are reading the book of Mark, they want to walk with Mark through his gospel. They want to get to know him. They don't feel they can teach his words without knowing something about the man himself. And it's the same thing with Jesus.

They want to walk with Jesus.

In many ways, the persecuted church has a much better, braver, more serious sense of the living character of God's Word. How many pastors in the West, in preparation for their sermon, have been struck by their complete inadequacy to teach a biblical truth? How many are scared of teaching a passage inaccurately? Some are not only taking the lazy way out of their responsibilities, they are also dangerously close to teaching heresy.

The absolute root of this issue in America is that we don't always trust the gospel; we don't trust preaching or prayer, which really means that we don't trust God to keep His promises. But God is sovereign in the saving of souls, and He does it through the gospel. Paul was crystal clear on this point in his letter to the Romans when he wrote, "I am not ashamed of the gospel, for it is the power of God for salvation to everyone who believes" (Romans 1:16).

While there may be things in the gospel we do not understand or that make us a little uncomfortable at times, it shouldn't
mean that we can no longer trust God to be there, or for the
gospel to adequately change lives. And none of these issues or
questions should ever mean that we should stop preaching the
gospel. The persecuted church has been given no alternative than
to trust God, and they do. They don't have high tech, or great
buildings, or the best music. They have God's Word and nothing
else, so they have learned to trust God . . . and each other. That
trust should exist no matter where God's Word is sown. And so
the gospel is preached, even in the midst of persecution.

THE PERSECUTED CHURCH has been given
no alternative than to trust God, and they do.

Brother Andrew has said, "If a message can't be preached
everywhere, it shouldn't be preached anywhere," so we need to be
mindful of possibly superficial interpretations of Bible passages
that reflect our compressed cultural bubble. There will also be
texts that will require a broadened awareness from one group or
the other to better understand the true meaning of the passage.

For example, Jesus concludes the Beatitudes during His
Sermon on the Mount with these challenging yet inspiring words:

> Blessed are those who have been persecuted for the sake of
> righteousness, for theirs is the kingdom of heaven. Blessed
> are you when people insult you and persecute you, and falsely
> say all kinds of evil against you because of Me. Rejoice and be
> glad, for your reward in heaven is great; for in the same way
> they persecuted the prophets who were before you. (Matthew
> 5:10–12)

Those in the persecuted church have a much stronger frame of reference for this passage. Believers who have survived the evil regimes of Pol Pot, Saddam Hussein, or Kim Il-Sung bear testimony after testimony to the surpassing grace of God in the midst of crushing trials.

Our Personal Perspective of the Gospel

But we also bring a personal, experiential perspective to the gospel. The temptations and challenges we experience rarely take the form of persecution, but they are temptations and challenges just the same. We are rarely in the position to choose our trials, but we can choose how we react in the midst of them. We must grow where we are planted.

Paul writes:

> No temptation has overtaken you but such as is common to man; and God is faithful, who will not allow you to be tempted beyond what you are able, but with the temptation will provide the way of escape also, so that you will be able to endure it. (1 Corinthians 10:13)

Peter echoes this concept of shared experience and endurance, while cautioning us to be ever on the alert:

> Your adversary, the devil, prowls around like a roaring lion, seeking someone to devour. But resist him, firm in your faith, knowing that the same experiences of suffering are being accomplished by your brethren who are in the world. (1 Peter: 5:8–9)

It is comforting to know that we are not alone in whatever trials we experience, and even more so that God is the one who will tend to our care when trials are upon us. But if we are to not just survive but thrive where we are planted, we must fully understand our surroundings, our opportunities, and our limitations. And, as we've learned from the testimonies coming out of the persecuted church, the fundamental limitation to our growth has little to do with our surroundings or our opportunities, and everything to do with the condition of our heart.

The Sower and the Seeds: Two Perspectives

In the parable of the sower and the seeds, Jesus—using soils and seeds as metaphors—describes four different heart attitudes and the way they respond to God's Word:

> Behold, the sower went out to sow; as he was sowing, some seed fell beside the road, and the birds came and ate it up. Other seed fell on the rocky ground where it did not have much soil; and immediately it sprang up because it had no depth of soil. And after the sun had risen, it was scorched; and because it had no root, it withered away. Other seed fell among the thorns, and the thorns came up and choked it, and it yielded no crop. Other seeds fell into the good soil, and as they grew up and increased, they yielded a crop and produced thirty, sixty, and a hundredfold. (Mark 4:3–8)

It is a well-known parable, so let's dig beneath the surface a bit. First, the main players in the drama are clear. As Warren Wiersbe has succinctly written, "The seed represents God's Word, and the sower is that servant of God who shares that word with others."[5] It is an interesting passage for all believers—both in the West and in the global church—for they can each act out two roles in the play. That is true for us as well, for at some point in every believer's life, the seed has been sown in our heart, but we are also called upon to sow the seed of God's Word toward others.

When we hear this parable, we most often think of ourselves in the role of the sower. We believe that God wants us to take His Word and throw it out along life's path. Sometimes we throw the seed and God makes it land on good earth. When it does, that seed will bear good fruit (i.e., the person we shared with comes to faith in Christ), and that's why God wants us to keep sowing the seed.

There is nothing wrong with identifying with the sower, for God does want us to share His good news. But our tendency to view ourselves as central to the story highlights how our Western "do-er" mentality tends to influence our thinking.

On the other hand, believers in the global church are most often drawn to consider the challenges presented by the different conditions of all four soils, but especially the two extremes.

When sowing the seed of God's Word, the persecuted church, especially in the Middle East and parts of Asia, often finds hard ground. In fact, up to 90 percent of the people they share the gospel with will reject it, both culturally and socially. It's an unpopular message in many cultures; it's a message of loss of family and friends, a message of stepping away from privilege into disfavor.

But where the soil is good, it is extraordinarily good. God's harvest in some persecuted cultures is often of the thirty, sixty, or even hundredfold variety. In some countries, despite the efforts of the government or the majority religion, the persecuted church is growing at a phenomenal rate. In recent years there has been a divinely appointed, supernatural harvest in China and India where the church has truly grown exponentially, all based on people hearing, and then trusting in His Word.

Dealing with the Shallow and Crowded Soils

The American church is faced more frequently with the other two soils—the shallow, or rocky, one with no root, and the crowded soil where the thorns come in to choke everything off.

In all frankness, our beliefs tend to be shallow. We hear the Word and often "immediately receive it with joy" (Mark 4:16), and as long as we feel delighted and excited and thrilled with Christianity, it's an awesome experience. But as soon as it becomes dull and repetitive, or as soon as we have to say no to our flesh, our greed, or our pride—when we have to confront and actually deal with the reality of our sin—we pull up our shallow roots and move on to something else that makes us feel better.

Shallowness is also at the heart of two serious issues in the West. Some elders and deacons—let alone the members and attendees of our American churches—can't explain such doctrinal truths as the two natures of Christ, or why the Bible is God's Word and the Book of Mormon isn't, or why we should understand the Old Testament and know how it fits with the New Testament.

Similarly, church growth via shallow soil can produce phenomenal greenery for a season. But fast growth rarely brings good fruit. If a new church plant explodes to one thousand attendees within a year, it may appear as if the soil is indeed fertile. In the case of the first-century church, time proved that the soil was fertile indeed. However, exponential growth may simply be the byproduct of an attractive charismatic leader combined with the "shiny bright new thing" syndrome. Like the first-century church, the test of depth is time and quality.

One good question to ask may be "How many churches in the area dropped from 350 to 200 to fuel that transfer growth?" Church growth should generally be a marathon run at a challenging but comfortable pace, not an all-out sprint.

So, while our shallowness manifests itself both theologically and in terms of true commitment, the global church can't honestly relate. Becoming a believer in a cultural pressure-cooker simply costs too much to settle for a lukewarm experience. They do struggle with other issues, but none related to shallowness. These believers have counted the cost to identify with Christ, and honestly understand what it takes to dedicate their lives to Him.

SCORES OF WHITE flags wave above the battlefield of life's daily struggles and disappointments.

The third soil, where the seed is eventually choked and crowded out by weeds and thorns, is also an unfortunate characteristic of the Western church, one that many of us can relate to. For all of its success stories, America is also a land of vast regrets, a country where the words "if only" could easily be embroidered on the white flag of retreat. Often scores of white flags wave above the battlefield of life's daily struggles and disappointments.

Sadly, many of us acknowledge that we have forgotten our first love. We know that worries and concerns over college tuition and second mortgages and job stress and family issues are choking away our intimacy with God. And yet we often stare, helplessly, as the Enemy steals away our joy.

Regrets exist in the persecuted church as well, although the things they perceive as weeds and thorns are quite different. A persecuted believer may feel choked by the temptation to compromise his faith under stress, or to not share food equally with other members of their community. Their lives are not as complicated as we've allowed ours to become, so they don't share the variety of ills and concerns that we do, but they do worry about the health of their children and loved ones. The deceitfulness of riches, a huge stumbling block to us, is rarely a temptation.

How to Survive the Hot Sun Test

There is a defining moment in the size and health of a church—and in the heart of every believer—that has everything to do with a dedication to following God's Word no matter the consequence. During times of trials or persecution, we must endure the hot sun test. Trials come to test our root system, to see if it can stand up to the withering heat of the hot sun.

And when the hot sun of adversity comes out, will the seed become scorched? Will it shrivel away because it lacks roots? Or will it take all the pressure and pain that the sun can bring to bear and use that heat as God's refining fire in order to grow exponentially and flourish?

A seed planted in good soil, with deep roots watered well by a caring gardener, will not only survive, but also thrive. When all of the other conditions are right, the heat of the sun will produce a marvelous crop.

Consider James's take on how to survive the hot sun test:

Consider it all joy, my brethren, when you encounter various trials, knowing that the testing of your faith produces endurance. And let endurance have its perfect result, so that you may be perfect and complete, lacking in nothing. But if any of you lacks wisdom, let him ask of God, who gives to all generously and without reproach, and it will be given to him. (James 1:2–5)

Following God's Word no matter the consequence is common among Christians in the global church; it should be an inspiration to us as well. Believers in some countries have often had to hide God's Word in their hearts and heads because it was unavailable in any other format. When the time is right, God has enabled them to call it forth.

After China's best-known pastor, Wang Ming-Dao, was finally released from prison, he said, "In these past twenty years, I have not had a copy of the Bible. Happily between the ages of twenty-one and twenty-four, I spent my time at home doing the housework and studying the Scriptures. I memorized many passages. These passages in my heart came out one by one and strengthened me. Had it not been for those words of God, then not I alone, but many others would have been defeated too."[6]

Over and over, the Bible encourages us to meditate on God's Word, for it is a living testimony of His holiness. This vital practice requires a lot of discipline, but as we've seen through the testimony of Wang Ming-Dao, it can also bring triumph out of tribulation, for ourselves and for others.

The psalmist knew this, and wrote a portrait of a believer who had clearly passed the hot sun test:

How blessed is the man who does not walk in the counsel of the wicked, nor stand in the path of sinners, nor sit in the seat of scoffers! But his delight is in the law of the Lord, and in His law he meditates day and night. He will be like a tree firmly planted by streams of water, which yields its fruit in its season and its leaf does not wither; and in whatever he does, he prospers. (Psalm 1:1–3)

When we treat God's Word with reverence, when we acknowledge that the Bible is the living, breathing Word of God and that its authority comes from Him, when we delight in His law and meditate on it day and night, we will be like that well-nourished tree planted by streams of water. We will survive the hot sun test.

And in God's name, we will produce a marvelous crop for His glory.

God is spirit, and those who
worship Him must worship Him
in spirit and truth.

JOHN 4:24

Pray for me that I not loosen
my grip on the hands of Jesus
even under the guise of
ministering to the poor.

MOTHER TERESA

2

Worship and
The Church

It's Sunday at 4:55 a.m. in Ho Chi Minh City. A capacity crowd has already gathered in a secluded house and courtyard accessible only by foot or motorbike through a labyrinth of inner city alleyways. The predawn time slot is nonnegotiable, for Sunday is not a day of rest in Vietnam's bustling, largest city. The men and women filling the converted private residence will disperse by 7:00 a.m. to start their workdays.

But this is not some underground political movement or a one-time promotional event. This gathering happens in the same place every week, and the same people participate.

It is a weekly church service, and at 5:00 a.m. sharp, it begins.

Despite standing-room-only conditions, everyone remains for the entire two hours. The service includes some communal hymn singing, but the primary focus is on teaching and reading from God's Word: nearly an hour and a half of speaking and exhortation. When the guest speaker—a pastor visiting from the West—concludes his talk after forty-five minutes, the host pastor rises.

"Since our friend has concluded early," he says graciously, opening his Bible, "I will finish out our time together."

Half a world away, many church leaders in the West are concerned with creating and executing services that will lure and entice people to come, using elements calculated to capture their attention, including large choirs, guest musicians, small orchestras, and an occasional dramatic or humorous sketch. Yet despite these efforts, and even though the services take place each weekend at the same times, many American churches have transient and rotating congregations.

In contrast, Christians in Ho Chi Minh City come to church because they yearn for it. It is the stuff of life. They don't come for themselves, or to be entertained. They come because they know they will encounter something much bigger: worship of the almighty God. They get caught up in it, they are refreshed by it, and they are renewed by it. They come to be right with God and to be with others who know they need the same thing.

Giving Honor to the Worthy One

In the United States, we tend to believe that worship happens in some sort of a "sacred" building once a week for about an hour, usually on Sunday mornings. The reasons people, seek out the experience vary. Some attend to refresh themselves during the week. Others go hoping to build up points with God through attendance.

The idea of going to church for God, of coming together with a group of like-hearted and like-minded people, can often be lost in the forest of felt needs. Maybe it's because we're playing to the wrong audience.

The Kennedy Center Honors Gala has become an annual highlight of the cultural year in Washington D.C. Originating from the Kennedy Center Opera House stage—home of the National Symphony Orchestra—the program recognizes up to five annual honorees from all the arts and salutes them one at a time from the stage using talented performers and colleagues from New York, Hollywood, Nashville, and the arts capitals of the world.

Although the Honors Gala always plays to a packed house of 2,300 spectators (and to millions of television viewers), the primary audience for each of these performers is a single honoree seated in the first row of the Kennedy Center balcony. While the award recipient looks on in delight, the entertainer on stage takes something created by the honoree—a song, a dance, a dramatic reading—and gives it back to them with a heartfelt and passionate interpretation.

That's a very limited picture of what it's like to focus our worship solely on God. No matter how many people attend a weekend service, if our worship is pleasing to Him, we have done well. And if it's pleasing to God—the only one truly worthy of worship—it means every need there will also be met at some level, and we have provided an avenue for God to do His work. So to ensure that our worship is pointed in the right direction, we need to save God a seat in the balcony.

VIBRANT CHRISTIANS see worship as life itself . . . an ongoing sacrifice to God.

Vibrant Christians see worship as life itself, something not limited by day, time, or place. They're worshiping when they're riding or walking to church as much as when they're in church. They're worshiping when they go to the office, not just when they carry their Bible through the church doors. Their life is an ongoing sacrifice to God. Their prayer is, "I am offering You my life today: the way I talk, the way I live. What You offer me is my best option, so I'm living my life out in a way that declares Your worth."

A prayer like that captures what pure and honest worship can and should be. The gathering of God's people on a regular basis is just a segment of their personal worship experience. Corporate worship merely gives a group of believers an opportunity to do together what they should have been doing on their own all week: worshiping God, in spirit and truth.

Worship, Unity, and Choices

If we allow worship to be locked up within the four walls of the church so that we are left on our own for the remainder of the week, we eliminate the potential for Christ to work through us and through our church body in the surrounding community. But God never intended for us to be Lone Rangers. Instead, we need to follow the lead of the global church and tear down the walls, permeate our culture, and make intentional connections in the real world. If the global church can do it with so much opposition, why is it often so difficult for us?

When we worship in and through our daily lives alongside a group of people who provide us with mutual love and support, we will be an influence in our culture.

We most often see that mutual support as vital throughout the week, but it is also fundamental during times of corporate worship. The apostle Paul writes in Colossians 3:16 that we should be "admonishing one another with psalms and hymns and spiritual songs." The persecuted church knows that worship is the lifeline that connects them to other people who are fighting the same challenges. And despite our differences, whatever they may be, we are called to come together in love for unity's sake.

In America, however, unity is frequently contrived. Our daily lives have become so compartmentalized that it is quite possible for us to live near one group of people, work alongside another, and attend church with a third. Our efforts at living together must improve if our worshiping together is going to be powerful in our consumer-driven society. The blame must be divided among the overabundance of choices we face outside of church and some-times within.

There is a dichotomy in all of this. America is known as the land of variety. Sometimes it seems as if everything we do requires us to make a choice, right down to the basics: paper or plastic? Coke or Pepsi? Ford or Chevrolet? Regular or decaf? But when it comes to corporate worship, our choices are limited because the majority of our churches only allow an hour and fifteen minutes for the program, and that program is scripted down to the minute. Each and every weekend, the pastor knows exactly how much time he has to deliver his weekly message long before he steps up to the pulpit.

SOMETHING VITAL MAY BE lost when worship becomes dominated by programming.

There is nothing wrong with following a theme or being pre-pared, but something vital may be lost when worship becomes dominated by programming.

As the visiting pastor speaking in Ho Chi Minh City discov-ered, time can be relative in the persecuted church. If he had asked how long the group in the house church wanted him to speak, they may not have even understood the question. In many parts of the world, a worship service is often an all-day affair. The congregation knows the pastor is finished when he stops talking and steps down. But it's never an issue. Many walk more than an hour just to meet with God and each other, and arrive early if at all possible.

There is very little structure: They pray, they sing, and they listen to the Word of God, often preached by more than one speaker. If they get hungry, they retrieve their bundles and break out their food. They usually have a regular teacher and a main Bible lesson, but much of the exhortation comes from one another where they literally go around in a circle or throughout the room and share. It is very participatory.

Worship That Is Organic

In the West, worship that combines teaching and active participation can be a lost art, so it should come as no surprise that our churches are often filled with spectators.

Authentic worship should be very organic. It should bubble up from life, not be imposed on life. We often get it backwards; we expect people to be filled up and then live accordingly. But God's Word says to live worshipfully, and *then* we will be more able to fill one another up.

It's much like the miracle Joshua and the Israelites experienced along the banks of the Jordan River as they prepared to enter the Promised Land. As they stood on the threshold of a new life after wandering in the desert for forty years, God commanded the priests to do something quite counterintuitive: His instructions were to take the ark of the covenant and step into the river, which was then at flood stage:

> And when those who carried the ark came into the Jordan, and the feet of the priests carrying the ark were dipped in the edge of the water (for the Jordan overflows all its banks all the days of harvest), the waters which were flowing down from above stood and rose up in one heap . . . so the people crossed opposite Jericho. (Joshua 3:15–16)

The Jordan River stopped flowing only after the priests got their feet wet, not before. In the same way, action on our part must often precede the blessing on His part.

The simplicity found in the global church flows naturally out of that approach. Unfortunately, it doesn't come as naturally to us. In fact, we often miss out on the simple things because we move past everything too fast. And yet the modern American church seems to have a desperate craving for simplicity—simplicity and authenticity that isn't forced upon us.

A generation or two ago, in many parts of America, Sundays predominantly meant church and a trip to Grandma's house for dinner, a leisurely time when the whole family just came together and talked. Today, in our modern culture, our Sunday schedules are filled before the day even begins. Sure, we make an effort to fit a church service in there somewhere—perhaps the true origins of the rise of Saturday night worship services—but then we're off to swim clinics, or soccer games, or dance lessons, or SAT preparation classes, and there's just no time for dinner at Grandma's.

Which doesn't really matter, because there's a good chance she's on vacation somewhere.

About Church Buildings and Worship

In the West, church buildings serve a dual function. They are built for marketing purposes as well as to house our congregations. Some church planners caution that we will not be recognized as a "real" church until we build the building, so until the building comes, the people won't. In other words, buildings create credibility.

In the memorable movie *Field of Dreams*, a farmer clears his cornfield and builds a baseball field after hearing a voice tell him, "If you build it, they will come." Perhaps that "Field of Dreams" philosophy—"if we build it, they will come"—has some credence in the West, but that's obviously not the case in the persecuted church, where buildings seldom exist, and where the peer-to-peer, family-to-family, neighbor-to-neighbor method of developing a church actually allows for greater simplicity, greater authenticity, and greater growth.

Consider the experience of the Ethiopian church a few decades ago:

> In 1982, the communists overthrew the government of Ethiopia and persecution of the church began. Along with other groups, the Mennonite churches had all their buildings and property confiscated. Many of the leaders were imprisoned and the members were forbidden to meet. The church went underground without any leaders, without buildings, without the opportunity to meet together publicly or use any of their public programs. While underground, they could not even sing out loud for fear someone would report them to the authorities.
>
> Ten years later, the communist government was overthrown, allowing this church to come out of hiding. The church leaders were amazed to find that their 5,000 members had grown to 50,000 in that ten-year period.[1]

Even the most pessimistic American church leaders would be overjoyed at the prospect of a tenfold increase in membership.

More recently—as part of the changing political dynamic in China—unregistered house churches in Beijing have sporadically been given permission to assemble in public. As you can imagine in a communist nation, the situation was very tenuous, but some churches have boldly taken the risk. One house church group in particular actually went so far as to take a lease on a large building, began to use it for their weekly worship services, and continued to do so for several months. However, during the winter following the Beijing Olympic games, with the world's eyes no longer laser-focused on their human rights policies, the dreaded government crackdowns began again. Their landlord, fearing possible repercussions from the government, locked them out of the building and told them they would have to go back "underground."

THOUSANDS OF BELIEVERS

assembled in the falling snow form a
visible symbol of how the persecuted church
doesn't require a building to survive.

But the first Sunday following the lockout, despite a heavy snowfall, the congregation chose to convene in the open air in the middle of a nearby city park. As the gathering grew from tens, to hundreds, to thousands of believers assembled in the falling snow, they became a very visible symbol of how the persecuted church doesn't require a building to survive, or to thrive, in the midst of government oppression.

Whether it's in a park in China or an alleyway in Tehran, on a hillside in southern Mexico or a beach in Sri Lanka, the church will continue to meet, serve, and worship, with or without a building. The persecuted church is not attached to any of the physical stuff that we get caught up in, often because they have nothing but God and themselves. But they also realize that those physical things may eventually become encumbrances.

When you spend a large percentage of your life on the run and in hiding, you learn to travel light.

What Is the Church? What Is Worship?

Perhaps one of the most important lessons we can learn from the persecuted church is a quick refresher course in our most basic vocabulary, especially if we're ever going to understand what God desires for us.

The word *church* is frequently misunderstood in the West. In God's dictionary, it has multiple meanings. The church is not always a building; in fact, in the New Testament Scriptures it's most often the people who choose to follow Him. When Jesus told Peter, "Upon this rock I will build My church; and the gates of Hades will not overpower it" (Matthew 16:18), He was not referring to any structure or architectural foundation. He was referring to His body, to the people who follow Him.

Another word is equally important, and perhaps just as equally misused. It is the word *worship*.

In congregations throughout the United States, the word *worship* has primarily become synonymous with corporate singing. When we refer to a "worship leader," we mean the person who leads and directs the musical portions of the service. But in God's terminology, the pastor should be considered a worship leader as well, perhaps even the primary one.

We need to relearn that in worship—even if we separate it between private personal worship and corporate gathered worship—*everything we do and say* is an act of service. Listening to the Word preached, prayer, the greeting time, the saying of the Apostles' Creed, the reading of Scripture, all these things are means whereby we are declaring the worth-ship of God.

And when that is understood, it should affect everything we do, especially our strategy.

In America, our worship strategies almost always focus on the form of the service: what the order will be, who's going to say what, what program elements will be used. In the global church, they talk almost exclusively in terms of function, and leave the form up to the organic movements of life.

It's hard for us not to focus on function because we link functionality with success. We are very much into what's effective, what's efficient. We love productivity and results.

In all fairness, the American church wants to be interested in relationships, but we often approach them the only way we know how: through lessons, seminars, and curriculum. After determining that our congregation is lacking in community, we conceive and develop a multiweek "relationship" series. Then we launch it with a "relationship" message on the weekend, perhaps featuring an expert or celebrity guest speaker.

But a year later (or five or ten years), how can we tell if people have developed stronger relationships if we are not in daily relationship with them? By what do we measure our results? What fruit do we expect to harvest? And how can we harvest anything if the trees aren't even planted in our garden?

The relationship question is huge in the modern church, especially in the next generation of believers. They want authenticity in relationships now. They attend our big structured services and say, "This is not authentic. We don't have any community. We don't have any real relationships." And they make a good point. So three or four people will meet together on a Sunday morning at a Starbucks and read their Bibles together and consider that church.

Some churches swing over to making participation in a small group the essence of church life—only to find that their people no longer understand and appreciate the corporate aspects of the body of Christ. Both are necessary, but even more necessary is that both be authentic representations of the heart and mind of Christ. If corporate worship degenerates into a spectator sport on the part of the attendees, and if small group life becomes nothing more than shared conversations about football, cars, and candles, neither one meets the New Testament standard of fellowship as "life on life."

The standard seminary answer to what the church is comes right out of Acts 2:42: "They were continually devoting themselves to the apostles' teaching and to fellowship, to the breaking of bread and to prayer."

THE CHURCH IS A GROUP of people who are regenerate; but there has to be leadership, sacraments, and mission.

Size doesn't enter into the equation. In the last chapter of Colossians, Paul talks about a church that meets in somebody's house, and then he talks about the churches of Galatia, so he delineates between the local church and the "universal" church.

Simply put, the church is a group of people who are regenerate; but there has to be leadership, and it has to be organized, and it has to have sacraments, and it has to have mission. The opposite is also true: if there are no sacraments (or ordinances), no mission, no outreach, no leadership, no church discipline, no preaching of the Word—the things that have always historically been the marks of the church—then it is not a church.

How Can We Be Authentic?

Another major point of discussion that often surfaces in the West revolves around the issue of church relevancy and authenticity. But a funny thing happened on the way to relevance; our definition of authenticity is primarily dependent on the generation that we're part of or ministering to. The use of a choir or pews or even a large building is not inauthentic by definition. When you talk to somebody in a retirement community, odds are that the phrase "authentic church" means a place you wear a tie.

Of course, the reaction against the "you've got to wear a tie" people is rooted in the new dynamic that has equated informality with authenticity. We have even witnessed the same thing in weddings. A wedding has traditionally been a noble, once-in-a-lifetime celebration of the beginning of a marriage relationship. Perhaps that is still the case in most parts of the United States. But in Southern California, more than a few couples have chosen to be married in jeans, followed by pizza at the reception—something that can easily reduce the ceremony to an everyday occurrence.

The persecuted church is not interested in "getting in step" with their culture. When they come together in worship, they are coming to an outpost of heaven; they are experiencing a foretaste of what it may be like to be standing before God's throne. They don't want to leave, because when they do, what they go back to is hell.

But it is too easy to talk ourselves into believing that our personal, private lives will bring as much satisfaction and edification as worshiping and fellowshiping with the body of Christ.

AUTHENTIC WORSHIP

... requires simplicity, unity, and community.

And the key to those three is humility.

As long as our primary focus is on ourselves, selfishness will divide us. Selfishness always does. If we come to church for ourselves, then it is easy to want to order our music and our preaching off of an "a la carte" menu. The only way a multigenerational church works is if everybody agrees that the mission of the church is outside the church. It has to be a community decision.

We must be dedicated to the call of Christ, not to the clamor of culture. After all, what is more important in God's hierarchy of

needs? It is the authenticity of our worship, which requires simplicity, unity, and community.

And the key to those three is humility. Richard Foster writes:

> Humility is as elusive as it is desirable. We all know that it
> can never be gained by seeking it. The more we pursue it, the
> more distant it becomes. To think we have it is sure evidence
> that we don't. But there is a way for humility to come into the
> habit patterns of our lives. Holy obedience opens the door. It
> is a central means of God's grace to work humility into us.[2]

"AM I FOLLOWING Christ, or am I just following the crowd that's following Christ?"

Truthfully, the theological definition of the church here and in
persecuted regions doesn't differ as much as the practical assessment of what the church is. In the West, the church is more of an
organization, an entity that gets things done, provides benefits, has
a building and an office, and is program-driven. In countries overseas where it faces ongoing persecution, the church really is a community. It's more like an intimate fraternity or sorority. Believers live
together even though they may not be in the same house. It's not
about whether they can come up with a program for their youth. It's
that families are just living life together.

Those of us in the American church must ask ourselves, "Am
I following Christ, or am I just following the crowd that's following Christ?"

In the persecuted church, they follow Christ. The personal
cost to follow the crowd is too expensive.

But there is something we must always keep in mind, whether
we are in America or in one of the most persecuted regions on the

planet; Jesus Christ is the head of His church. Everywhere. And despite our differences, in most ways we are all in the same business and the same family, pursuing the same mission under the same head. So even if the American church is somewhat crippled in certain areas, it's still His church. Not ours. And He has every right to remind us of those things that we need to improve. His church has never been perfect throughout history, and yet He still chooses to work through it, and through us. It's the number one vehicle through which the kingdom mission is being forwarded today.

And no matter where a church is located, the key is getting leadership who understand the mission and who know that God is the primary audience of worship. It's not just about sending people out with smiles on their faces.

It's about making sure that God is pleased.

But I say to you, love your enemies and pray for those who persecute you, so that you may be sons of your Father who is in heaven; for He causes His sun to rise on the evil and the good, and sends rain on the righteous and the unrighteous.

MATTHEW 5:44–45

3

Prayer and Dependence

The Yalu and Tumen Rivers form a naturally meandering boundary between The People's Republic of China and The Democratic People's Republic of North Korea. The two rivers, flowing from the Changbai Mountains in northeastern Asia to the northern shores of Korea Bay, are shallow and heavily silted for much of their length. Yet they are much easier to navigate than the political lines they help delineate.

Night and day, soldiers from both armies stare vigilantly at each other through high-powered field glasses as they control traffic in and out of their respective countries. Those approaching the Chinese checkpoints find that travel moves at a snail's pace, for each is high risk and high security, and very few people are allowed to cross the heavily fortified border regularly. Behind the Korean border, the situation is not much different. There are checkpoints everywhere. Traveling inside North Korea is almost impossible.

But one man does go around the country. To those of us in the West, he is known only as "The Traveler." He is one of the persons who helps Open Doors distribute goods inside North Korea. Despite the ever-present danger of exposure, The Traveler remains an unpretentious and simple man. He looks more like a blue-collar factory worker than the Korean James Bond, but that's one of the keys to his success. He's adept at blending in, remaining both vigilant and decisive.

It's a matter of survival.

He has served Open Doors for years, and yet we don't even know his real name. We never will. The fewer people who know it, the better, for if his secret work on behalf of God's people were ever to be discovered, it would mean a brutal death sentence for him.

The Place of Prayer inside North Korea

When Open Doors leaders spoke to him, we asked him what the church in North Korean prays for. This ostensibly emotionless man who puts his life on the line every day—often for people he's never even met living in cities he's never visited—began to weep.

He told of a church movement that has remained underground ever since the fifties. In order to wipe Christianity from the face of the land, Kim Il-Sung's soldiers herded entire congregations into the streets and ran them over with bulldozers. Thousands of men, women, and children—nearly all of them North Korean citizens—were literally crushed to death, their remains compacted, recycled, and used to line roadbeds throughout the surrounding cities.

Today, under Kim's son Kim Jon-il, there are between two-hundred thousand and four-hundred thousand believers, direct descendants of those who were left behind. And when they pray, The Traveler said, theirs is a prayer of repentance.

Ironically, their genuine and sorrowful penitence doesn't correlate to anything they've done personally, nor is it even rooted in a tragedy of their generation. Instead, it grows out of a collective sentiment that their grandfathers were not bold enough witnesses during the years of the Japanese invasions, and later during the communist takeover. They feel as if the punishment of communism for the last sixty years has been because their ancestors did not speak out enough, and they live with such an intense, inherited guilt that they actually view as a daily reminder from God to not compromise their faith.

And they deal with that daily reminder the same way they do everything else: with prayer.

It's simple. Believers in North Korea—and those throughout the persecuted church—don't see prayer as an add-on activity. It's not like they have a relationship with God *and* they pray. Theirs is a praying church, and their relationship with God is a prayer relationship. It is completely integrated in a way that ours in the West just isn't.

To them, prayer is simply communion with God, and they have a wealth of experience that we have seldom tasted, or enjoyed the benefit of. When they come together for corporate prayer, it's almost sanctified desperation. Someone leads out, and then everyone in the room prays, passionately, often multiple times.

They pray for things we probably wouldn't think to pray for, and never pray for many of the things we do.

THEIR PRAYER IS a prayer for liberation. . . .
They pray for Kim Jong-il's salvation.

Much of our prayer comes in response to a dutiful call to improve our lax spiritual disciplines. We're supposed to pray in our church services, so we do. We're supposed to pray for our food, so we do, quietly and quickly, especially if we are out in public. We rarely *have* to pray out of a sense of dependence, and so we often don't. Admittedly, few people in the West even "like" to pray.

The question of "enjoying" prayer never comes up in other parts of the world.

North Korean believers are prayerfully focused on one purpose: to be in place and fulfill God's will for their lives. Their prayer is a prayer for liberation, for lifting of the darkness, for a possibility to reopen the churches of their ancestors, and for reconciliation. They pray for Kim Jong-il's salvation.

So despite the dangers, The Traveler continues to equip believers with commentaries, Bibles, radio resources, training, and encouragement to keep them focused on the Lord. In a country where a church is completely underground and believers rarely meet, believers often pray alone, but they pray with one voice.

The Traveler knows that if there's ever going to be freedom there, it will be because of prayer. Already, Christians are free in Christ.

Dependent versus Self-centered Prayers

Whether we admit it or not, how we view prayer is one of the primary indicators of how we view God. If our philosophy puts man at the center of the universe and God as the one who simply provides blessings and benefits, then our prayer will be, "I need something, and this is when I want it and what it should look like." But in cultures that are under the iron fist of dictators and despots—something most in the persecuted church have in common—there is a clear understanding of a vast power that no one can withstand. They see the dark side of that power every day of their lives, but it helps them comprehend an even greater power for good that is found in God. So they come before Him in great dependence and great humility, genuinely thankful that they are allowed through God's grace to actually commune with the creator of the universe.

By contrast, prayers in the Western church are often selfish and me-centered. Christians here tend to transform God into the great benefits-provider-in-the-sky, and Jesus Christ becomes their personal assistant. It is too easy for Americans to treat Him as if He were on retainer. We pray for logistical or situational things, rarely anything tactical or strategic. And we're often too busy or too rushed to pray for very long.

If we pray or study the Bible for the purpose of leveraging God to help us improve business, lose weight, or not get sick, that's self-centered. But if we do it for His glory, then prayer and study begins to work on our hearts. It enables us to see life in a different way, through a different lens. We start to realize that the person next door needs God as much as we do, and that prayer is how you unlock even the most cynical of hearts.

A heart focused on self will remain hardened, but it is softened and broken through suffering and through a genuine concern for others.

But the prayer of the American church is not a brokenhearted prayer. It's a prayer for our rights—what we deserve or what we should have. And sometimes it even grows into a demanding prayer. The prayers heard from persecuted Christians are the prayers of a broken heart concerned only with conformity with God, rather than asking God to meet us where we are.

How are they able to get it right? The vast majority of believers in the global church have learned how to pray directly from reading and hearing Scripture. To them, prayer is not some quaint religious practice handed down from their parents or their pastors, and it shows. The prayers of the persecuted church are much like David's. Reading through the Psalms, you get the idea that prayer *is* desperation; it is pain and anguish but also thankfulness for God's presence

Vietnamese Pastor Cuong, who spent six years in prison for his faith, says this about prayer:

"In my work I was so busy I had no time to pray. But in prison, I was thankful to God that he gave me time for prayer. I had about six hours of prayer every day. I had time to recall every member of my congregation to pray for them. Before that, although I served the church, I didn't have enough time to pray for them. I learned about the real presence of God [in prison]. When you kneel down and pray wholeheartedly to the Lord, you feel his answer right there."[1]

Compassionate and Authentic Prayers

Two Iraqi refugees were asked recently, "How can we pray for you?" Their responses were both unselfish and mature, and provided a great model for us to follow. One said, "First pray for those who are doing the persecuting," an amazing response considering that he and his companions had recently lost all of their material possessions. Some had even lost loved ones. The other man said, "Pray that we would have our dignity restored," because they were still trying to find how God was going to use them—and how He would make them whole again—in the midst of a terrible situation.

Toward the end of the conversation, they said, "Our prayers are continually before God," a clear reminder that our prayers are not to be a short episode or performance, or even a laundry list of personal needs, but instead a continuous communion in God's presence. Theirs are prayers of compassion for their enemies and communion with their Father.

In many ways, an immature and flawed approach to public prayer has diminished the effectiveness of prayer in America. Instead of communion with our heavenly Father, it has often become a performance. Believers in the global church do not pray to perform. They really depend on it as a lifeline, something to which they cling tenaciously.

To be effective, our prayers must be genuinely authentic before God. But we are rarely comfortable being authentic with each other, so we find it difficult to be authentic with God in prayer. Granted, part of this communal nature in the global church is cultural. In many nations, especially those under persecution, believers live so closely together that there's no concept of privacy. Everybody hears everything anybody says.

But even our private devotions in America tend to be from the head rather than the heart.

In Colombia, however, and in many other parts of the globe, devotional times are centered on communal prayer. There is time for reading, study, and preaching, but believers there lean heavily on their personal connection with God, and with each other. The nature of the persecuted church is such that many have no access to the written Word. The life of a believer in many parts of the world requires them to go to God from their heart, not from their head.

WE CAN ASK PASTORS and lay leaders from the persecuted church what one disciple asked Jesus, "Teach us to pray."

One of the challenges the persecuted church faces is an enormous need for training. Pastors often have little or no formal experience, yet are responsible for the spiritual development of tremendously large groups of people. Every chance they get to communicate with pastors in the West, they ask, in complete humility, "Teach us how to teach. Walk us through the Bible so we can do it with our people."

Theirs is an absolute heart dependence on prayer. We need to follow their humble example and ask their help. We can ask pastors and lay leaders from the persecuted church the same thing one disciple asked Jesus in Luke 11:1, when he said, "Teach us to pray."

Humility, Authenticity,
and the Lord's Prayer

If our prayer is to become one of humility and authenticity, calling a very consumer-driven and prosperous nation back to God, we would be wise to turn to the Lord's Prayer (Matthew 6:9–13).

"Our Father who is in heaven, hallowed be Your name" is the belief in whom and where God really is. The character of God doesn't change, whether we live in good circumstances or bad. The persecuted church knows this, and they frequently turn to worship when they have nothing else. God doesn't need our praise, but we need to praise Him. It is how we acknowledge His sovereignty. Praise is our way of telling God we will wait on His righteousness and His timing, and that we entrust Him with our very lives.

Voices lifted in praise during times of trials are just one testimony of our faith in His sovereign power.

"Your kingdom come. Your will be done" is an understanding and acknowledgment that our primary allegiance is to God's kingdom, not to a government, not to a political party, not even to a political ideology. The allegiance of every believer should be to God's kingdom, and our prayer should be that His power through the Holy Spirit and through His church would transform society.

The phrase, "Give us this day our daily bread," is directly tied to the New Testament command to be generous. The apostle Paul says, "Instruct those who are rich in this present world . . . to be generous and ready to share, storing up for themselves the treasure of a good foundation for the future" (1 Timothy 6:17–19). The whole point of giving isn't because God needs the money. It's because by giving we discipline ourselves to say, "My hope and security are not based on what I have. I'm going to give you some of it, and it shows me that God will supply me with what I need."

But even when we do give, something subtle can easily happen to get us off track. In American consumer-driven churches, tithing is often pitched as an investment strategy by which we can get a better return, rather than allowing God to teach us that we don't need more; we simply need Him.

In truth, giving is not for God, or for God's work. God will do His work, and He doesn't need us to accomplish anything. Instead, giving is for the entire community. Read the book of Acts. The early believers shared a common fellowship. That meant that those who had, shared equally with those who did not have. In Christ, it was no longer about what you could get. There have always been "haves" and "have-nots" in church fellowships, but the point is not to elevate the rich, or even to elevate the poor. The point is to have "in common" with one another, and the church that has in common is an unstoppable church.

It won't be unstoppable because it's on multiple radio stations, or because it has ten thousand people coming to the weekend services. It will be unstoppable because the hearts of the people are full of generosity for those in their midst as well as those on the outside of their fellowship.

Sacrificial giving is God's way of reminding us that our dependence is on Him and not on our stuff. That's what the persecuted church has. They live with dependence, they live with the ability to say, "Give us this day our daily bread," and mean it, because they're never sure where it will come from, or when. All they know is it will come.

But our barns are often full, and we need discipline.

"Do not lead us into temptation." In America, we're not only fine with temptation, we like to live far out on the bleeding edge of it. We don't easily recognize the daily vulnerability we have to Satan's activity. But he is constantly blinding the minds of the unbelieving and he is producing counterfeits. This phrase means, "Lord preserve me from all of the counterfeits that Satan is ever throwing before me: counterfeit security, counterfeit success, counterfeit gospel, counterfeit Jesus, and counterfeit church."

We need to be firm in our faith so that we don't sin.

"Forgive us our debts, as we also have forgiven our debtors." We struggle with forgiveness. Many of us simply don't know how to forgive, and others have no desire to learn. To some, forgiveness equates with weakness.

In the persecuted church, forgiveness is simply a nonissue. They have a more fatalistic approach to life. In the words of the old pop standard song, their approach is often "Que sera, sera, whatever will be, will be." It may seem completely absurd to us, but when you've been part of a society that never offers justice, injustice is not even a blip on the radar.

WHEN WE ARE PRAYING to not be led into temptation . . . the real prayer is for our heart to be delivered from a love of evil.

Christ's prayer that the Father "deliver us from evil" reminds us that evil pervades this world. Its reach into our lives is far more subtle and insidious than we give it credit for. The worst evil that men do is not from an external source; it's from an internal working. And the deliverance from evil can't always be associated with an external legislative or social agenda; it has to be done at a personal heart level. So when we pray not to be led into temptation, not to give in to temptation, not to play around the temptation, the real prayer is for our heart to be delivered from a love of evil.

This is the portion of the Lord's Prayer that the persecuted church offers up most often on behalf of American churches and believers. One Chinese pastor put it this way:

"We really pray for you in America because you're confronted with a challenge that external persecution doesn't rise to the level of. Materialism and the subtle attacks of the enemy from the inside are in many ways more debilitating to the believer and to the church than the external."

He's right, of course. If we are attacked externally—as our nation was during the tragic events of September 11, 2001—we galvanize and draw strength from one another. But an internal enemy is much more subtle. Our blessings can easily become vulnerabilities because they can get us sidetracked. Materialism, affluence, and all of the other things that invade the American church and cause divisiveness are much more difficult to fight against because they seem so natural and normal.

Daily Devotion to God

The Lord's Prayer has always been a morning prayer, meant to be spoken daily. So when it says, "Deliver me from evil," it means "Deliver me from evil *today*." And that has been true from Genesis 3:15 on, when God said that there was going to be an ongoing enmity between those who followed Satan and those who followed God. And that enmity—the idea that the opposition party knows who we are and doesn't like us—presupposes that we are so conspicuously righteous that we would be the targets of unrighteousness.

When we flippantly pray, "Deliver us from evil," we almost certainly don't realize that the phrase is a clarion call for us to remain so conspicuously righteous that the evil principalities of this world really would hate us and do everything in their power to undermine us. Based strictly on our behavior, it can be difficult to discern the differences between those of us who know Christ and those who don't.

Jesus said, "You will be hated by all because of My name" (Matthew 10:22), and few would argue that Christ-followers are not popular in many cultures around the world today. But unfortunately, that enmity is rarely for the right reasons.

The persecuted church is a day-by-day deliverance church. It is a church that requires daily communion with God. These believers depend solely on God for their daily bread, and for daily deliverance from evil.

The real prayer is for our heart to be delivered from a love of evil.

GOD'S HEART DESIRES constant contact, so that He can daily integrate His will into ours.

In many ways, we've become a weekly church, primarily for an hour and a half on the weekend, traffic and parking time not included. And, because we've become accustomed to our week-to-week episodes of experiencing God, any prospects we had of basking in His daily-ness have simply evaporated. Our prayers are few and far between.

But God's heart desires constant contact, so that He can daily integrate His will into ours, and our will into His. And yet that conformity of our spirit that comes from daily dependence on God—a conformity that the persecuted church understands so naturally because of their external circumstances—has simply been moved aside.

Prayer should be the crucible shaping our lives into conformity with God, through a daily relationship with God. Prayer literally should be pouring our lives out before Him. This is something that the persecuted church gets absolutely right.

If there is one word that severely limits our prayers, it's when we add the preposition *for* instead of *about* to our questions. We ask, "What do you want me to pray *for*?" as opposed to, "What do you want me to pray *about*?" This isn't just semantics. That one word change creates the false understanding that prayer is all about asking.

We are told to bring our requests forward, so we do the adoration and confession and thanksgiving to "soften God up" for our supplications. We want to prove to God that we are faithful to Him as He is faithful to us. But look again at the prayers in the Bible. David's are heartfelt cries from an anguished soul full of deep contrition for sin.

Prayer is an opportunity for us to come before God with open and honest hearts, knowing that we really don't have the right to be there.

IF GOD OWED US an answer to any of our prayers, then we'd be in charge.

God doesn't owe us anything, and the key to prayer as dependence is simply realigning our understanding of who God is. The persecuted church understands that God is the only one to whom they can turn, precisely because He doesn't owe them anything. If God owed us an answer to any of our prayers, then we'd be in charge.

In Revelation 2, the church in Ephesus was caught in the crosshairs of a sad truth, one that could easily be written about the church in the West: "I know your deeds and your toil and perseverance. . . . [You] have endured for My name's sake, and have not grown weary. But I have this against you, that you have left your first love" (Revelation 2:2–4).

Returning to our first love will require humility of mind and humility of spirit. It will require an approach to God that requires authenticity when we pray, "Give us today our daily bread. Don't lead us into temptation *today*, and deliver us from the evil that's within us *today*."

Each component of that prayer should remind us to approach God with fear and trembling, on our knees, weeping, recognizing all those things that we so quickly move past in America.

Behold, how good and how
pleasant it is for brothers to
dwell together in unity!

PSALM 133:1

Let him who until now has had the
privilege of living a common
Christian life with other Christians praise God's grace from the
bottom of his heart. Let him thank
God on his knees and declare: It is
grace, nothing but grace, that we
are allowed to live in community
with Christian brethren.

DIETRICH BONHOEFFER

4

Community, Culture, and Evangelism

For all of its benefits, the automobile has done more than its share to diminish the reality of community in America. It's not just because of the high cost of gas and insurance. Before the horse and buggy gave way to faster and larger versions of the horseless carriage, our towns and neighborhoods were self-sufficient. Each city, village, town, and hamlet had a neighborhood grocery store, a neighborhood hardware store, and at least one neighborhood church. Weather permitting, families walked to church and knew everyone else who did.

Today, we can put our kids in the car and travel forty-five minutes or more to shop for a church. There we hope to find the exact sort of "experience" we want, even though it is miles away from our neighborhood and our neighbors.

A Lesson from Addis Ababa

In Addis Ababa, the capital in Ethiopia, only a privileged few have access to automobiles. Most citizens can afford to ride buses or share taxis only to get to work. Their neighborhoods consist of hundreds of shack-like dwellings, many with shared walls. Folks really live together, and they most often travel together. To help overcome the transportation issue, churches are spaced no more than five miles apart—many being much closer—because that's how far people can comfortably walk. And since the majority of the citizens live in one of the city's many shared neighborhoods, they walk to church together.

For them, community is where they live every day, it's where they work and sing and play and help each other and live life together. Their church fellowship is a clear extension of that. Here everything is viewed in the context of the family and community.

For example, in an American Christmas pageant, we expect to see Mary and Joseph depicted as traveling to Bethlehem alone on a donkey. But when the same event is dramatized in Ethiopia, the scene includes Joseph and Mary and their entire families as well, because it's unimaginable in that culture for a man and his pregnant wife to undertake a 110-mile journey alone.

No wonder there was no room at the inn.

A Lesson from American Housing during the Twentieth Century

In all fairness, this modern phenomenon reaches far beyond the church. It permeates our culture.

Those who study twentieth-century American residential architecture, for example, have spotted an interesting trend. Houses at the turn of the century had large front porches and detached garages, often placed near the back of the lot. As the decades passed, the porches grew smaller and garages grew larger. Around the midcentury mark, the garage became attached to the house, and the front porch disappeared.

Today, we drive up in our cars, open our automatic garage door, drive in, shut the door behind us (after turning off the ignition, so as not to asphyxiate ourselves) and enter the house through the garage.

We don't have to see or engage with anybody outside of our houses. We're not forced to talk to our neighbors, let alone get to know them. In fact, the average American often knows more personal facts about their favorite entertainment and sports stars than they do about the families living next door to them.

And yet we desire connection, because God designed us to be in community. And genuine community is a scarce commodity in today's culture.

A Longing for Companionship

Many are familiar with the phrase, "Absence makes the heart grow fonder," but absence can also make us long for the companionship of people we don't even know.

Consider this: If you've ever traveled abroad, especially to a country or region where English is rarely spoken, you know how exciting it can be to run into someone from "back home," a fellow citizen who speaks your language. And even though your ability to communicate with each other may be the only thing you have in common, it is as if you are both suddenly part of an ancient brotherhood.

Yet once you're back home, surrounded by the comforting sound of familiar words and phrases, if you saw the same person on the street or in the mall, you probably wouldn't even glance in their direction.

Scarcity adds value, even to relationships.

Creating Community among the Generations

So how does the modern American church develop and nurture true community? Community develops through familiarity and commonality. And so much of it really goes back to how we view the family unit.

Church leaders talk about wanting to be multigenerational, yet often attendees do not spend time with their family members while they are in a church service. In the old denominational church model, there wasn't any child care. There was church, then Sunday school, and then a repeat of the church service. You could go to church and then Sunday school, or Sunday school and then church, but it was always one or the other, so the family unit was together at least half of the time.

Later, because infants distracted many people (including the pastor) during the message, many churches added a "cry" room, complete with rocking chairs, a glass window, and soundproofing so as not to disturb the congregation. This may have increased the peace and quiet in the worship center—if indeed that should be a church value—but it leads to a kind of purgatory for moms. In fact, the cry room may be the closest thing to a smoking area you'll find on a modern church campus.

WHEN WE BREAK UP the body of Christ by age range, we end up with a fractured church.

Today, we divide out more than just the infants. We've hired experts to take care of all of our kids, from youth ministry to AWANA, and many churches even offer a service for "mature" adults, where the congregation can happily sing hymns without causing a stampede toward the exit doors.

But when we break up the body of Christ by age range, we end up with a fractured church.

Some American congregations are bucking this trend and offer child care only for infants through age three. The remainder of the children and youth remain in the service through the congregational singing and announcement time before they head off to their respective classes.

Here's the main issue at stake: Many children—even those from active, churchgoing families—have no sense of what it is like to go to church and sit with their mom and dad during the service. On the few occasions it actually happens, it's a weird experience for the kids and the parents.

The experience is even stranger than it should be, of course, because young people don't spend much time with their parents the other six days of the week either. And this isn't an isolated issue; it affects all economic classes across the board.

In affluent areas, nannies and domestics handle many of what used to be the "parenting" chores, and in single-parent or dual-income families, the kids are often left on their own. Even in more traditional households, challenges remain. Today, families don't often eat dinner together, even if everyone in the family is at home. When families stay separate by choice—and when parents don't spend enough time with their kids—both sides lose. Parents don't get to know who their children really are, and parental absence can make it difficult for the kids to learn to relate to adults, or even understand what it means to be one. And that may lead to other challenges and consequences down the road.

American parents tend to discipline more actively the younger the child is, and less as the children grow older. Maybe it's because they just get worn down. In the Chinese and Indian cultures, it's the opposite. In China and India, the kids are all over the place, running and jumping. But teenagers are respectful. They talk to you, and they listen. Our kids are often forced to be quiet until they are teenagers, and then they're off to the races.

Parenting does not provide instant gratification, which is perhaps why Americans have such a struggle with it.

When the American church takes on the characteristics of the modern American family, many of those characteristics involve selfish, immature, shortsighted, "me-first" decisions. Worse yet, believers often avoid making decisions altogether. They want to keep their options open. To use the old male-female dating argument, they are "scared of commitment" to the body of Christ. Even before they choose to marry and have families, their patterns reveal this attitude: They may attend a weekend service at one church, belong to a small group at another, and perhaps check out the hot new "singles night" at a third.

AT TIMES CHRISTIAN parents seem
to simply mirror those who don't follow Christ.

And after they choose to marry and have families, what do dads and moms choose to do when they have free time? Fathers often hang out with their buddies instead of with their kids. Moms sometimes put the family on "autopilot" and insist on a weekly "girls night out." At times Christian parents seem to simply mirror those who don't follow Christ. In part because of their parents' confusing example, American kids often try to escape the house any way they can to hang out with their friends.

If they're not careful, these parents may end up like the father in the Harry Chapin song, "Cat's in the Cradle," a man who was always too busy for his son, until he realized the reality too late.

This is one area where small churches have a distinct advantage. Like the vast majority of communities in the persecuted church, they eat and socialize together, often because they enjoy each other's company, but sometimes because it's harder to hide in a small church. When only sixteen families attend, every new family that comes in gets noticed—and enfolded—right away, whether they want to or not!

Sadly, the global church is being adversely affected by our Western mind-set. We go overseas and tell pastors that they need to build a building (if they can) with one room for adults and one for kids, and that they've got to start their children on their own curriculum program.

Even though we mean well, our strategy appears to be more "divide and conquer" than "build up."

Because of their cultural traditions, their lack of resources, and their preference for being rather than doing, the global church is already multigenerational—something we say we aspire to—and should be allowed to stay that way. Their kids don't know any other way to do life. Their entire life experience is multigenerational. And they don't grow up with the expectation of being entertained. They simply participate along with everyone else.

Even when we do make connections at our churches, we need to be intentional about our relationships. Getting together to socialize is a great start—certainly in our culture—but we must be careful of letting our fellowship end there. We need to follow the example of the early church in expressing true oneness, says Reuben Welch.

There is a fundamental difference between the fellowship of Christians and Christian fellowship. Too often we are together as Christians doing the things we like to do together—volleyball, parties, teas, leagues, receptions, and whatnot. Or we get together and talk about cars and sports and babies and clothes and weather and Sunday school attendance and we come away having talked and laughed and enjoyed ourselves. (But) it does not deepen the oneness of the fellowship to multiply such activities. These things do not express oneness, but the study of the Word does, the sacraments do, and prayer does. We need to be together more doing the things that really give expression to the common life we share."[1]

We need to grow together, not just socialize.

A Theology of Community

Scattered throughout the New Testament are more than forty "one-anothers," instructions to the early church from Paul, James, Peter, and John on how to best live in community. These run the gamut from positive reinforcement to outright exhortation. For example, "Love one another" (Romans 13:8), "Submit to one another out of reverence for Christ" (Ephesians 5:21 NIV), "Admonish one another" (Colossians 3:16 NIV), "Offer hospitality to one another without grumbling" (1 Peter 4:9 NIV), and "Do not slander one another" (James 4:11 NIV).

When we use these and others to construct a theology of community, we see that God's plan for how we act and operate in society is all about the "one anothers." The persecuted church gets this. Their community of fellow believers is often the only place they can turn to for help and assistance. But here's the dilemma for the American church: In order to really practice the "one anothers," you have to be with one another. You have to be together in situations that you can't escape.

For example, the admonition to "forgive one another if any of you has a grievance against someone" (Colossians 3:13 NIV) pre-supposes that we are going to have relationships with people in our church communities who upset us. But if we don't have to see or be with such individuals on a regular basis, it becomes a nonissue. Or, to bring it closer to home; if we can easily divorce that person, or if we can go to work and leave the kids with somebody else, there's no "one another" involved, but there is also no growth or learning.

Dietrich Bonhoeffer, the martyred German pastor who knew a great deal about persecution, explains God's intent for placing us alongside challenging brothers and sisters in Christian community:

Our community with one another consists solely in what Christ has done to both of us. . . . The more genuine and deeper our community becomes, the more will everything else between us recede. . . . If we do not give thanks daily for the Christian fellowship in which we have been placed, even where there is no great experience, no discoverable riches, but much weakness, small faith, and difficulty . . . then we hinder God from letting our fellowship grow according to the measure and riches which are there for us all in Jesus Christ. . . . Christian brotherhood is not an ideal which we must realize; it is rather a reality created by God in Christ in which we may participate.[2]

Transients at Heart

This aspect of our culture radically affects our community mind-set. In our culture, we are trained and conditioned to be transients at heart. Simply put, no matter what we are doing or where we are in America, we know we can always leave. It is one of our inalienable rights. But in the persecuted church, people know that odds are great that they will never live more than a half mile from where they were born.

If we know that we can just drive to another church next weekend, if we can pick up and move to another part of the country if we want or need to, that awareness can make a big difference in our approach to community and relational commitment.

When the going gets tough for us, the not-so-tough can just hop in their cars and leave.

Part of this restlessness may be due to our relative inability to see or—to be more accurate and honest—control the positive outcome of remaining in community in challenging times, or doing the hard work of parenting. Like the culture we often mirror, we have become addicted to outcomes. Much of what we do is tied to a specific result.

In America, if you go to a party, the first thing you are asked is, "What do you do?" This whole mind-set affects the church in many ways. Not only do we equate activity with success—which helps create a dependence on outcomes—but also because when what we do becomes the measure of our success or our worth, we tend to lose value as we grow older, which brings about the subtle ageism issues discussed above.

The global church knows that a relationship is not measured by any outcome; for example, they don't go to their husbands or wives and say, "We want to be among the best families in our community, so let's go through our checklist to make sure we hit our objectives today." That's almost a parody of what a real relationship is.

But that's what God called us to do within the church and in our communities, to build relationships for His glory.

Relationships Versus Resources

Here's the rub. Because so many of our efforts at relationships revolve around programs and related resources, it is easy to ask ourselves, "How well did we use the resources we were given to accomplish something we think is important?" And, truthfully, that is a fair question. But relationships and resources are two different things. If you lack resources, as they most often do in the global church, you never worry about the outcome.

In the underground church in China, for example, they lack the choices that we have. They have few choices about anything, and must rely on relationships and community to get through each day. But because we do have choices, it forces the question, "What would we need to forego in order to have that kind of authentic community?" It doesn't make sense to simply give up our resources, because God does use them. A large church with a staff of eighty-five can provide services to the family and to the

community that a church with eighty-five attenders cannot provide. We acknowledge that.

A SAYING AMONG African Christians
sums up this challenge: "In America,
you have watches. Here, we have time."

So if we must make a change, it must be in the area of
improved interdependent relationships.

The persecuted church understands interdependency
because they rarely have any other support structure. When
somebody in the persecuted church says, "Please pray for me
because my mother and father are kicking me out of the house,"
they are truly seeking prayerful intervention from their community right then, not a halfhearted promise to consider their dire
situation if it comes to mind again.

That may seem like an extreme example, but those situations
occur quite frequently in the persecuted church. Believers are at
risk each day of either being discovered by a family member or by
someone else. In China, believers will place food on a table and
decorate it as if they are celebrating someone's birthday just to be
able to meet in public. We can't imagine having to do that kind of
stuff merely to gather in Christian community.

But when we're part of a community and we're dependent
on that community, we become willing to risk things that we
wouldn't have imagined risking before. And it always has much
more to do with relationships than it does with resources.

The only resource the persecuted church seems to have more
of is time. Obviously, they have the same number of hours that we
do, but we fill up our time to the absolute limit. There is a saying

among some African Christians that sums up this challenge very neatly: "In America, you have watches. Here, we have time."

Sometimes, however, Americans do recognize the need to slow down, to get away. And when they do, they tend to choose one of two extremes for their vacations. They either go to a resort to live for a few days at a lifestyle level they can't possibly attain, or they go completely in the other direction, back to the simple life. But staying at a posh resort, although refreshing, can make them even more envious of what they don't have. A journey back to the simple things, however, is often more satisfying.

There is an echo in our lives that longs for that simple, soul-satisfying, no-frills relationship. We get glimpses of it when our family or our close group of friends is together and relaxed. It's the same sort of feeling we get after finishing a satisfying meal.

That feeling is an echo of the original image of God.

SURPRISINGLY, WITH ALL

of their challenges . . . the global church
has that peaceful level of satisfaction.

If we were given some truth serum, we'd probably admit that during those peaceful moments when time stops, when we feel a connection with our brothers and our sisters, that's God at work. Surprisingly, with all of their challenges and painful experiences, members of the global church have that peaceful level of satisfaction. In fact, that might be the most surprising lesson to be learned from the global church. Through their example of quiet strength under pressure, and in pain, they inspire us to pause, to slow the pace of what we're doing.

Consider your response when something painful happens.

You stop whatever you're doing, right? If you're running or walking and your knee gives out, you have to stop. The pain forces you to stop and adapt a very slow and measured pace.

Similarly, when the pain and suffering occurs regularly within the persecuted church they choose to live at a different pace, a pace much closer to how God intended us to live. In contrast, we in the West frequently choose to numb that pain with a variety of painkillers. We attempt to move past pain as quickly as possible, and as a result, we miss out on so much of what God wants to teach us. Because of their measured pace of faith and life, those in the global church are able to celebrate the simple things of life better, deeper, and longer. And those things lead to stronger communities.

Community Contact without Compromise

Unfortunately, we can't bring simplicity back without throwing out all the handholds that our society has created over the years. If we try to create a completely "other" community in the midst of our fast-paced, success-oriented culture, we run the risk of appearing (or even becoming) cultlike. But because one of God's intentions for Christian community is to be inclusive rather than exclusive, to be available to our nonbelieving neighbors, we have to find ways to simplify our lives without making outreach impossible.

Pastors love to preach out of Acts 2, because it provides such a vivid picture of a church that really understood what it meant to be in community. Everybody sold their land and shared things equally. But fewer pastors teach from 2 Corinthians (at least not that same weekend) and talk about what happened later when Paul went around to all the Gentile churches, taking up a collection to help support the believers in Jerusalem who had sold all their stuff, and now had to get help from other people to meet their needs.

God doesn't want us to go back and be the first-century church; that's not what we were called to emulate. God wants us to be a loving, caring, community-oriented church in the twenty-first century. He wants us to be salt and light to our neighbors today.

To be effective, salt has to have a connection with that which it preserves, but it can't lose its saltiness. We have to have contact without compromise. That is the balance we need to seek today, but it's a big challenge for us: holding the tension between contact and compromise.

If we have no contact, we become like the isolated, insulated fundamentalists who want nothing to do with anybody who disagrees with them, who are not allowed to have friends who are nonbelievers. But if we have no contact with nonbelievers, how are we to add to God's church?

On the other side of the spectrum—if we have total, full-immersion contact, we run the risk of developing lives rife with compromise. Some churches and Christians want so badly to influence the world that they minimize the important distinctions they have with them. In that scenario, we may start changing their stance on "hot-button" moral issues, or become involved in politics for all the wrong reasons. We may begin appreciating the finer things in life—the things that only money and influence can buy—because we enjoy those things. But as we become more and more like the world we're trying to reach, we become ill-equipped to deliver the message that God offers something different for us in this life.

Some say that adopting the lifestyles of our culture becomes a bridge to the unbelieving world. But through the past several centuries, the ideas, theology, likes, and stylistic preferences of unbelievers have had much more of an influence on the church than the church has had on them.

"IN THE WEST, we are not persecuted. We are intimidated."

In other words, we may have discovered a bridge to the unbelieving world, but most of the traffic is moving one way.

In all honesty, our culture is not hostile to us. Even at its most aggressive, it's not very hostile. The founder of Open Doors, Brother Andrew, has put it succinctly. "In the West," he says, "we are not persecuted. We are intimidated."

On the other hand, the persecuted church experiences a hostile culture every day, and doesn't worry about pleasing it. They don't give in to that pressure to adapt. They believe that they have been saved from that culture, so why should they want to go back?

With the absence of any real—rather than perceived—cultural pressure, the Western church can be lulled into a false sense of spiritual security, allowing us to become slowly shaped by our culture, sometimes unknowingly. The concept out there of an "evolutionary hermeneutic," for example, teaches that as culture has evolved, the Bible has evolved and become more complex along with it. The proponents of this concept start with examples such as slavery and polygamy, which were once accepted by the church, but now they are not. But then—for one example—they extrapolate to the changing role of women, but based on an inaccurate interpretation of Ephesians 5, the text that supposedly promotes the subjugation of women.

Studies such as these gain ground in the Christian community simply because the American church wants to be seen as being in step. We don't want to appear as that which culture would hate. It's just like the seventh-grade boy who comes to school wearing a white T-shirt, but sees that everybody else is wearing blue T-shirts. When he comes home, he asks his mom to buy him a blue T-shirt, because he needs it to fit in. And that's what we are doing with an increasing frequency. There's absolutely nothing wrong with buying and wearing a blue T-shirt, but there may be an issue with what actually drove the purchase. In the shadowy areas of subtle culture influence, the most important question to ask is usually not "what," but "why."

This cultural confusion has everything to do with how we study and accept Scripture. The global church doesn't have an overriding intent to fit in with culture so that they may reach them. Instead, they say, "We are going to be people of the book, and we will live according to the book, and we believe God will save those around us through our lives and through the gospel—not whether we wear blue or white T-shirts." And that has everything to do with how they treat and revere God's Word.

WHEN WE CLAIM allegiance to God's kingdom but . . . bend to fit into the culture, we are hypocrites by definition.

This uncertainty alone—and ultimately, this weakness—is really why the Western church is so open to ridicule by the culture at large, because once believers cross over into the kingdom of Christ, they *do* become aliens to the culture. They must. So whenever they act in accordance with the kingdom, the culture condemns them. It must. But the hypocrisy comes in when believers attempt to act just like the culture or allow the culture to define the norm for them. When they do, the culture says, "Wait, you said you were different. I don't believe in your God, but you said that you do. Why don't you act like it?"

And the sad reality is, in those moments, culture is absolutely right.

For when we claim one thing—in our case, allegiance to God's kingdom—but live according to another—when we bend to fit into the culture—we are hypocrites by definition. And when this happens, we are wide-open to the criticism we receive.

The criticism that the persecuted church receives is drastically different, almost the polar opposite of what we receive. They are considered counterrevolutionaries in communist countries, and infidels to the teachings of Muhammad. They are persecuted for following God in lands where He is not worshiped. But our culture condemns us for being hypocrites, as lukewarm as the church in Laodicea.

How Should We Care for This World?

Perhaps you have seen the bumper sticker that tells other drivers that we are "not of this world." Christians see it as a reminder not to have our treasure on earth, which is a good thing. But unbelievers may read the message differently. To them, it may say, "I don't care about your environment, I don't care about your governmental or cultural problems. This world's not my home, so I'm treating this planet like a hotel room."

And you know how people frequently leave hotel rooms.

In America, the younger generation is attracted to "social justice" issues; much good is being done in the United States and around the world. There are so many needs and ways to serve: from fighting human trafficking in Asia—as well as in major cities in America—to digging wells in Africa and providing shoes, mosquito nets, and wheelchairs, to teaching job skills in third-world countries. Through these and other service projects, Christians are able to illustrate how we can be the uncompromising hands and feet of Jesus as we come alongside nonbelievers to serve the real needs of our brothers and sisters around the world.

And the world is noticing such acts of Christian compassion.

When it comes to caring for those in our communities, we must be careful of withdrawing, of thinking or saying, "This culture is going to hell in a handbasket, and that's why we're not involved." This view may be perceived as a subtle disregard for our communities, our nation, and our planet. It's not something that we say in so many words, but we often show it in our actions, and in the way our churches are structured.

That's another thing we can learn from the persecuted church: the value of priority and perspective. They live in the here and now. That is true in all aspects of their lives, even when it comes to their theology.

The persecuted church is not so much interested in being delivered out of this world. They are more concerned with demonstrating within the confines of this world, and that makes living in this broken world bearable and endurable.

A Message That May Alienate—
or Transform—Your Community

The late Francis Schaeffer spoke and wrote of how we are at liberty to change the "form" of our churches, but not the message or the function. So pastors and churches are left with the question, "How much like the culture should we be? How estranged from the culture should we be?" We have padded chairs, we have air-conditioning, and we try to do music that is accessible. We are at liberty to adapt to the culture except in the message and the function of our church. The danger comes when we adapt the message to the culture because we are afraid of offending people.

In a well-known passage found in Acts 17, Paul stood up before a crowd in Athens—the center of the cultural world at that time—and said: "For while I was passing through and examining the objects of your worship, I also found an altar with this inscription, 'to an unknown God.' Therefore what you worship in ignorance, this I proclaim to you" (Acts 17:23).

Then he began to tell the gathered crowd all about God and Jesus; next, he presented the gospel. But the Athenians did not react like the Ninevites who accepted Jonah's delayed message to their king. Many sneered at his message about the resurrection of the dead. Only a few in the crowd said that they wanted to hear more. Fewer still joined Paul, so few that the book of Acts even lists some of them by name.

Let's put this episode in a modern-day context. Imagine that you are invited to lecture to a group of one thousand faculty and students at a major secular university. You give them the story of the promise of Christ in Genesis 3:15, and how it's worked through the Old Testament, and about Jesus, and redemption, and the application of righteousness through faith. And, when you finish, 997 of them rise from their seats, mumbling disparaging remarks as they exit. But the remaining three come down to the front of the classroom and each say, "You know, I'd like to hear more about that." Would that be a win for you?

Paul thought so. He thought so that day in Athens, and throughout all the days of his ministry.

But with Paul, even in the midst of the ultimate cultural plurality of religion that Greece had, he never made an angry appeal. He simply said, "You guys seem to be really religious around here, and I just want you to know a little about the real God that you don't know about." In light of the intellectual capacities of the crowd in that day, everyone would have understood that his message was a clear challenge.

But it wasn't designed to infuriate, it was designed to be clear. And that's where we can easily get off track.

Paul understood the difference. He wrote:

But thanks be to God, who always leads us in triumph in Christ, and manifests through us the sweet aroma of the

knowledge of Him in every place. For we are a fragrance of
Christ to God among those who are being saved and among
those who are perishing; to the one an aroma from death to
death, to the other an aroma from life to life. (2 Corinthians
2:14–16)

We have to ask ourselves, "Why are we here?" The answer is
always the same. We are not here for ourselves; we are here to
magnify the glory of God. And sometimes magnifying the glory
of God will turn off our neighbor.

And God's okay with that.

First of all, then, I urge that entreaties and prayers, petitions and thanksgivings, be made on behalf of all men, for kings and all who are in authority, so that we may lead a tranquil and quiet life in all godliness and dignity.

1 TIMOTHY 2:1–2

Courage is not simply one of the virtues, but it's the form of every virtue at the testing point.

C. S. LEWIS

5

Leadership, Authority, and Power

Today Pastor Chen (not his real name) remains one of the principal leaders of the burgeoning house church movement in China. Now in his midseventies, he has weathered several revolutions, both political and social. And, as you may expect for a leader of a religion largely deemed illegal by his government, his journey has not been an easy one.

Although his mother was a nominal Christian, he kept her faith at arm's length for years. As a young man he earned an advanced degree in physics, took a teaching position at a leading Beijing university, and joined the Chinese communist party. Then, at the onset of the Cultural Revolution, he and thousands of other Chinese intellectuals were sent to work in a factory where they were required to read and discuss the *Little Red Book*, and worship its author: Mao Zedong.

Because of his natural philosophical bent, Chen soon came to the conclusion that Mao was not worthy of worship, and informed his factory superiors that he was no longer interested in the practice. For that simple statement—not because of a profession of faith in anything else—he was sent to prison, where he remained for several months. One day, in great despair, he made his way to the roof of the prison building, intending to commit suicide. As he swung his leg over the low wall surrounding the roof high above the prison yard, he heard a clear and distinct voice saying, "Don't do it; I have plans for you."

When he turned and saw that no one was there, he instinctively knew—in part from his mother's early influence—that the voice he'd heard was that of Jesus. Standing alone on that prison rooftop, he gave his life to Christ.

When the Cultural Revolution ended, he was released from prison, and was reinstated to his Beijing professorship. Throughout the 1970s and 1980s, he had many opportunities to share Jesus. But although he was very open and candid about his faith, and was respected as a favorite educator, few students were interested.

"I would talk to my students day in and day out," he remembered, "and they would mock me. 'Oh, Chen, you know God's phone number; would you give him a call for me?' 'You know, Chen, you're a great professor, but you don't get it.'"

The Search for Democratic and Religious Freedom in China

By the late 1980s, the social idealism of these students that had simmered for so long finally boiled over. They wanted democracy and believed in a political solution. Many had hoped that Secretary General Hu Yaobang, who had long been a proponent of rapid political reform, would help usher in the change they sought. But in January of 1987, Yaobang resigned under duress, and the government forced him to denounce his reform policies in a humiliating public "self-criticism." When he died suddenly of a heart attack on April 15, 1989, the sad occasion provided a perfect excuse for students to gather in massive groups, not only to mourn, but to bring renewed attention to their growing pro-democracy protests.

Student and teacher boycotts of university classes were soon followed by hunger strikes and demonstrations, all of which led to a May 20 declaration of martial law. Because the military's entry into Beijing was blocked by thousands of protesters, the army was eventually ordered to withdraw on May 24.

By the first of June, thousands of young people had begun to gather daily in Tiananmen Square as a visible sign of their waning faith in the government. Revolution was in the air. Perhaps spurred on by similar dissident rumblings in Germany and Eastern Europe, which would lead to the dismantling of the Berlin Wall five months later, students from the Central Academy of Fine Arts erected a beautifully carved statue of the Goddess of Democracy, a decidedly political—not religious—deity.

"CHEN, WE WERE WRONG.
We thought politics was going to be the answer. Tell us about God."

Pastor Chen visited the square along with several of his students in early June. He still has a photograph of himself posing in front of the Goddess of Democracy statue.

The date stamp on the photo reads June 4, 1989, the day the tanks rolled in.

"The whole city was paralyzed," he recalled. "People came in from all over to witness and be a part of what was going to take place. But as soon as the square was filled, they closed off the streets and brought in the tanks."

Although there has never been an accurate count of the dead and wounded, most reputable sources agree that thousands died in Tiananmen Square and in other parts of Beijing that infamous day. Pastor Chen remembers the event vividly, but also what happened in the weeks and months that followed.

"Several days later," he said, "the students who had survived came back to me and said, 'Chen, we were wrong. We thought politics was going to be the answer. We thought democracy was our hope for the future, but we see now that it has no meaning for us. Tell us about God.'

"All of these young intellectuals who were disillusioned with politics completely turned to Jesus Christ. God used that disillusionment to start the house church movement in the universities. Those young men are now the generation that's leading the movement forward."

Pastor Chen had sown the seeds of truth for decades. But instead of taking on the Chinese government, he patiently waited until the political solution ultimately failed. When his students finally sought him out, searching for real hope, he was ready to teach them something new.

When Chen talks now, he shares an immense vision of the Chinese church. But because his homeland is so vast, so diverse, there will always be more than one China, and more than one type of church. Much of that has to do with geography. Without question, the large cities and urban areas are embracing rampant and roaring capitalism and new levels of religious freedom, but in the fringes, in the poor areas, and in the vast open spaces of the interior, the communist government continues to maintain absolute totalitarian control.

Because of this dichotomy, any discussion about the liberalization of Chinese policy can be challenging and confusing. An argument can easily be made that restrictions have been loosened in Beijing, Shanghai, and other big cities, but if you travel to Tibet and ask the Christians there if China is a liberal democracy, you'll receive a completely different answer. Tibetan Christians are currently at the bottom of the pecking order in that region, and are persecuted by every other people group that lives there. Tibet is still an incredibly harsh place for a believer to exist.

TIBET IS STILL an incredibly harsh place for a believer to exist.

Hundreds of Christian evangelists, many from rural areas, remain in Chinese prisons for no other reason than sharing their faith in Jesus Christ. Sunday school meetings are still routinely broken up, especially in the far provinces when government officials can easily get away with it.

And so it goes with persecuted believers across the globe. Despite everything from atrocities and deprivation to social stigmatism, downtrodden Christians maintain their faith with remarkable patience and daily devotion. More amazingly to the Western mind-set, they do so compliantly. For other than in Iran, where there's a strong link between the spiritual revolution and the political revolution, the vast majority of those victimized for their faith do not undertake any serious or organized attempts to change their government. In fact, many are as proud to be citizens of their countries as we are to be Americans. The Chinese yearn only to be godly people in China. Even many North Koreans— among the most persecuted Christians alive today—share a strong national pride.

Daily, intentionally, and through God's grace, those in the persecuted church are attempting to do what Paul wrote in 1 Timothy: Live a tranquil life, don't make waves, fly under the radar, follow as many rules as you possibly can without disobeying God.

But this lifestyle choice creates a huge paradox: In most of these countries, believers are—by legal definition—breaking the law by professing to believe in Jesus Christ. Even in countries where believers are not directly persecuted for their faith, life can be extremely complicated.

The Search for Religious Freedom in Egypt

One Egyptian professor who converted to Christianity in his midtwenties experiences this daunting dilemma firsthand.

When you are born in Egypt, you are issued an identity card with your religion permanently stamped on it, and it's against the law to change your religion there. In the West, we consider religion to be a personal choice, a conviction, not an identity such as being of Irish or Italian descent. But in Egypt, religion is viewed strictly as an identity.

If you're born to Christian parents, you'll always be a Christian. If you're born a Muslim, you'll remain one until you die, at least according to the law.

Even though it is legal to be a Christian in Egypt, it is illegal to change religions, so the status on this man's ID card remains "Muslim." When he fell in love with a Christian woman with a Christian ID card, things became even more convoluted. He couldn't legally marry her, because mixed-religion marriages aren't recognized under Islamic law. The Christian church they attended eventually performed a ceremony, but they had to do it secretly. Now, his children face an even bigger issue. Because religion follows the father's lineage in Islam, they're legally considered Muslims, and have been issued Muslim ID cards, even though they have been born to, and are being raised by, two practicing Christians.

Don't misunderstand; neither of these believers would complain if their government changed the law. They just don't choose to take an active role in making that change occur. Even though they know their union will never be recognized under law, and that their children will have to endure similar challenges, they carry on, trying to live a tranquil life, following as many rules as they possibly can without disobeying God.

This biblical attitude is an inconvenient and definitive challenge to the church in America. Our nation's very beginnings grew out of rebellion against the legal authorities of our nation. It was primarily economic; we had experienced taxation without representation and weren't very happy about it. But free-market capitalism is not the only biblical approach to economics. If you examine the persecuted church, they are largely socialist in practice. Everybody has to share everything, because they have so little.

And culture tends to follow economics, even in the area of faith.

Limits to Political Power

In our culture, we tend to view power as the best way to achieve anything, and attempt to use the government as a mechanism to aid us in the preaching of the gospel. In other words, if we can somehow get the legislature to make a law that will force my neighbor to be a better person, or at least one in our likeness, it would be a wonderful thing.

But working only through an outside agency such as the government can make us relationally lazy, which can clearly limit our accountability to influence change on a personal, one-to-one human basis. And the simple fact remains that, in a democracy, laws can be changed.

For example, in the 1980s, many political conservatives tried to combat culture by legislation, and won some hard-fought battles. Then, in the first ninety days of President Bill Clinton's administration, nearly twenty years of social achievement in areas such as abortion—much of what had been accomplished by administrations of Presidents Ronald Reagan and his successor,

George Bush, and celebrated by the Moral Majority—was eliminated through executive order.

Paul wrote that power is perfected in weakness. Not that we should choose weakness, but that we should understand we *are* weak. He was given the thorn in the flesh not to make him weak, but to make him realize how weak he was. But in America, our long experience with freedom allows us to think that flexing our legislative muscles will somehow be better for the kingdom. We need to wean ourselves of the addiction to power.

It was addictive to the first-century church, too, and that's why Paul emphasized how God's power is perfected.

CHRISTIAN POLITICIANS
operate most effectively as dam-builders, and churches as seed-sowers.

The simple truth is sometimes our personal political agendas align with God's, and sometimes they don't. Instead, the determining question for individuals and churches should be "How is the kingdom of God going to benefit from my actions?" There is a not-so-subtle danger in having a dual allegiance. The persecuted church is singularly focused on the mission of Christ through the gospel. Most don't even consider changing the government because they don't have—never have had—the political muscle to make it work. The fact that we have perceived political muscle tends to drain our vitality as we spend resources and time to try and do mission work through legislative means.

In America and elsewhere, Christian politicians operate most effectively as dam-builders, and churches as seed-sowers. Both jobs are necessary and important. Christian politicians can hold back the waters of negative change, but they can't change culture long term. However, while they're holding back the waters, it can make it easier for the church to sow the seeds.

But when the church becomes overly involved in building dams, nobody is left to sow the seeds.

The global church recognizes that if God wants to change the heart of the king or dictator, He can and will. Their agenda is not political. It is not designed to promote democratic capitalism around the world. It is designed for individual believers to share their faith, one by one, with their neighbors and coworkers who don't know Christ.

The Personal, Grassroots Approach

Not long ago, the leadership team at Grace Baptist Church in Santa Clarita, California, was interviewing a young man to be a junior high pastor. As part of that process, one of the leaders asked him to share his proposed program for evangelism. Instead of saying something they expected to hear, like, "I'm going to go out to the schools to lead evangelistic Bible studies," the candidate said, "I believe the best way to reach kids is for kids to reach kids."

The room grew quiet.

Finally, one of the elders said, "You're right. I guess we were looking for you to be the man who would do that, but your idea makes more sense." That's because the candidate's answer comes straight out of Ephesians, where Paul tells pastors and teachers that their job is "for the equipping of the saints for the work of service, to the building up of the body of Christ" (Ephesians 4:12). If pastors to adults are called to equip the saints for the work of ministry, why should it be any different for those who serve in junior high?

The grassroots nature of one junior high student sharing the gospel with another junior high student in language they both understand is much more powerful than the junior high pastor telling the student.

The persecuted church maintains the same grassroots mentality. Most people have heard the phrase, "all politics is local." In the regions of the world where faith-based harassment is most active—where churches are forced to meet in secrecy—believers know to their core that evangelism and all of church life are local as well. They're not concerned about numbers. They don't ask the government to help them from the top down. They do it from the ground up, every day.

It's a refreshingly New Testament philosophy. It's "loving your neighbor" with a capital *L*.

THEY WILL KNOW we are
Christians by our love, not by our laws.

Recently, at a conference in Madrid, a missionary who works among Muslims described the way he and his coworkers operate. They start by making contacts in the dice rooms in downtown Marseille, France, where Muslim men—primarily immigrants from North Africa—spend their days playing dice.

"We are there every day," he said. "We learn each man's name, we practice our Arabic with them, and sometimes we teach them a little French. Through experience, we've determined that it takes at least 150 contacts to turn a Muslim acquaintance into a friend. Then, through the gospel, we pray that God will turn our friends into believers. When He does, we work with the believers to make them fully formed disciples who make contacts of their own."

The persecuted church is growing not because they have the

power in the capital city, or the freedom to hold big open-air crusades. It's because one Christian working in a factory next to a non-Christian has a different quality of life, has a different connection to meaning and purpose, has an understanding that makes the other person thirsty.

In the words of the old song, "They will know we are Christians by our love," not by our laws. If we align ourselves too closely to the legal side of things, it can make it very difficult to be as loving and gracious as God calls us to be.

Learning Limits in India: The Cases of Dhiren and John

India prides itself on being the largest democracy in the world. It's not at the top of the list of countries where religious persecution runs rampant. And yet, in certain states and regions throughout that vast nation, political leaders continue to allow discrimination against Christian religious practice.

Dhiren Dagal is a twenty-year-old Indian citizen from Orissa, on India's eastern coast. He is also a practicing Christian. In August of 2009, his tailor shop was set on fire and destroyed by a mob of Hindu nationalists during a wave of violence precipitated by the murder of a Hindu swami. Eyewitness accounts confirm that police stood by and watched while these mobs ransacked the village. Even though Maoist Marxists claimed responsibility for the murder months later, days and nights of violence and rage were completely focused on the small Christian community there.

Dagal lost much more than a shop in the riots. As he ran home after unsuccessfully fighting the fire, he came upon a horrible scene.

"They had tied both my mother and father to a tree," he said. "They raped my mother in front of me, and then set both of them on fire." His parents did not survive the torture, but he and his brothers were able to flee their village to the nearby jungle, going days without any food, medical care, or shelter.

"I've lost everything," he said. "I lost my family and my home." His prayer request was simple, and profoundly stirring. "Please pray I can continue to be a strong witness for Jesus Christ."

When we imagine the stories of those who are persecuted for their faith, we often visualize one such as Dhiren's, accentuated by violence, hatred, and impoverishment. But the persecution of God's people wears many faces, so the battle against it must take many forms as well.

Interestingly, the relatively few occasions that legal channels are utilized to combat persecution take place in countries that claim to be democracies.

John Dayal is a Christian activist. Formerly a journalist with the Delhi edition of the Indian newspaper *The Mid-Day*, he was renominated in 2010 as a member of the National Integration Council, Government of India, a group chaired by India's prime minister. He is also Founder Secretary General of the All India Christian Council.

For more than four decades, Dayal has exposed and investigated thousands of individual and "structural" cases of human rights abuse, including violence and deprivation specifically aimed at minority groups (including Dalits, Muslims, and Christians), and is dedicated to fighting organized human rights abuse across India and beyond.

Unfortunately, Hindu extremists see the conversions of Dalits (often referred to as the "Untouchables") as destructive to the caste system and the Hindu power base. Because Dayal's influence is felt worldwide, his life has been threatened on several occasions by these groups and others.

Still, despite his many challenges, Dayal remains dedicated to fighting organized human rights abuse across India and beyond. And, although he uses all of the legal means at his disposal, he is also continually working to strengthen the relationships among the many groups.

We may be moved and horrified by Dhiren Dagal's story, but the faith challenge John Dayal faces each day is much more similar to what we experience in the West. Although our lives may not be directly threatened like John's has been, we face largely internal battles. We may chafe under ridicule or feel threatened on occasion by social ostracism. Meanwhile John has walked the path of more resistance. Even though the beatings he experiences come verbally or in print—rather than through the sticks and stones variety—they can be painful.

Moving beyond Politics

Even in democracies such as India, the persecuted rarely choose formal government channels as a primary tool for seeing the church established and built up in their country. When less than 10 percent of the population identify with your religion, advocacy is largely ineffective on a political level.

Conversion is often complicated in India. Christians need to apply to local authorities to convert, and are questioned to ensure that the conversion wasn't coerced through food or money enticements. In many cases converts are forced to reconvert under local or family pressure, abuse, torture, or even death threats. These are not idle threats, as thousands have been persecuted in this way in the year 2010 alone.

Christian believers can't get enough votes to make it legal to be a Christian convert in any of these situations, and they recognize the practical limitations of it. But they also recognize that a spiritual dynamic is lost when you go toward law. It's easy to take God out of the equation, when in reality He is the entire equation.

In contrast, because we think the Western church is thriving, we enter into the public arena with the presupposition that we're doing God's work. And we easily slip into the mind-set that God probably supports the politically conservative party. Our logic is simple: Because God opposes abortion, He must also support conservative financial policies. But here's the flaw in that argument: You can just as easily make a case that Jesus was a liberal. After all, He fed a whole lot of people for nothing.

It's too easy for political conservatives to say that their opponents on the other side of the aisle have abandoned biblical Christianity, but the truth is, good-hearted people get distracted on both the left and on the right. The persecuted church teaches us this lesson: Stay simple. Stay individual in our methodology, and we'll stay a lot closer to the message of Jesus.

FOLLOWING A POLITICAL agenda
gives us many reasons to be divisive,
even among fellow believers.

Following a political agenda also gives us many more reasons to be divisive, even among fellow believers. It's too easy to get caught up in and become competitive with the "other" side. We need to repent of the fact that we have not done enough to address the root causes of our moral and social decline.

Admittedly, those who have lived their entire lives under any level of persecution have a more fatalistic approach to life. When you've been part of a society that doesn't give you justice, you don't worry about injustice, just as fish don't notice that they're surrounded by water. In our culture, we always expect justice, and that's why we struggle when we're slighted.

But those in the persecuted church realize that true justice is ultimately delivered in heaven. In the midst of their trials, they get to that place a lot quicker than we ever would. Their reaction is almost always that they can remain a bold witness for Jesus Christ. We'd want to have the justice questions answered first, to have our rights protected.

Proper Prayers for Our Leaders

In 1 Timothy, Paul writes to encourage his young friend to stand firm as a pastor in Ephesus, and he encourages the church there to pray for all kinds of men, including kings and authorities (2:1–2). It just so happens that the folks who were being asked to pray were the oppressed minority in that region, and the people they are being told to pray for were their political oppressors. The original readers would have understood that God was leading them into some dangerous situations, but that the mission of heaven includes all kinds of men.

And so they prayed for their enemies, and waited on God.

We read that text today and often imagine a totally different context. We make the argument that God wants us to pray for our leaders for their individual salvation or for the good of the country, because if they become saved they'll be better people. But do we pray for them so that God will be glorified in their life, or so they'll become more like us? We ought to pray that the mission of Christ would be bigger than the political mission of our party, and the mission of Christ is to save souls.

We make a show of praying for our government, but sometimes we pray almost in a vindictive way. We pray that they would get it right, that God would so change them that they would then align with our political philosophy. In all honesty, there are times in the persecuted church when people are not praying for their government, when they're lamenting about what is taking place and that their government allows mobs to do the terrible things they do. But those prayers are like David's words in the Psalms, anguished cries to a loving Father, seeking justice, but ultimately leaving it in His hands.

In the book of Daniel, God did change King Nebuchadnezzar's heart, but Nebuchadnezzar still destroyed Jerusalem. Clearly, God was less interested in maintaining a political kingdom than He was in reaching—and changing—the hearts of His people.

We can try to blame our impotence on everything from materialism to denominational distractions, but the real lie that the church has bought into is that power brings influence. The people who turned the world upside down in the book of Acts had zero political power. They were always in the minority.

You never read a prayer in Acts that talks about the Roman oppression. You never read a prayer that says, "We need to get better emperors or better laws or more Christians in the senate." It's not that it would have been a bad prayer; it's just that it would have been a completely ineffective strategy.

Greater Power for Change

Like Paul, those in the persecuted church absolutely believe that the power that raised Jesus from the dead is the greater power. Sometimes it seems as if the church in America no longer trusts God to do God's work. We don't trust the kingdom power. We don't trust preaching in America anymore. We don't trust the gospel. Worse, some in the church have changed the gospel to be self-centered because they worry that if we really told people, "you are a sinner," our churches would soon be empty.

If we objectively examine the tactics of the church over the last twenty-five to thirty years, it appears as if we have adopted a belief system that says if we get the laws right then we will be conformed to God, and we'll return America to the way God intended it to be. But the problem with any kind of alignment between evangelicalism and any political agenda is that over time the ethic of the political agenda may become dominant.

IF OUR CHURCHES were full of people who choose to live transformed lives . . . political divisiveness would become irrelevant.

So God chooses to work primarily through the human heart. If our churches were full of people who choose to live transformed, heart-changed lives, who reach out into their communities on an individual basis to influence and enlighten society, political divisiveness would become irrelevant. In times of revival, prisons didn't cease to exist; they just sat empty. Following the great revivals, people just didn't do the things that put them in prison. We don't need more laws in America. Heaven knows we have enough laws.

There is an old adage that states in the absence of the internal control of behavioral constraints, the only thing that maintains civil society is external controls. In other words, where character is lacking, you need laws to constrain evil behavior.

President John Adams wrote, "This constitution is only fit for a moral people. It's wholly inadequate for anyone else."

The problem arises when character goes almost entirely lacking. In that situation, the new ethic becomes "whatever is legal is right; whatever is illegal is wrong." And in this context, abortion is now "right" in America because it's legal. And the ironic statement of the left, that you can't legislate morality, becomes absolutely true.

Probably the most famous prayer is the Lord's Prayer, and a

central part of it is, "Let your kingdom come." If God's kingdom really did come, issues such as abortion would be pushed aside. Truth and morality would reign because they glorify God, not because they make America a better place to live.

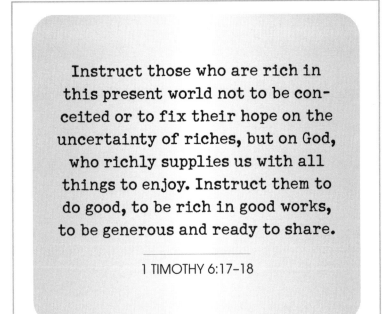

Instruct those who are rich in this present world not to be conceited or to fix their hope on the uncertainty of riches, but on God, who richly supplies us with all things to enjoy. Instruct them to do good, to be rich in good works, to be generous and ready to share.

1 TIMOTHY 6:17–18

6

Generosity and Stewardship

Beginning in August of 2006, the official currency of Zimbabwe—the Zimbabwean dollar—began a collapse as precipitous as any in the latter half of the twentieth century. Launched in 1980 to replace the Rhodesian dollar, the Zimbabwean dollar (Z$1) was introduced with an exchange rate comparable to 1.47 American dollars, which placed it in the upper echelons of world currency.

However, continued political turmoil and hyperinflation soon took their toll, and in 2006, the Zimbabwean government officially announced that their new currency going forward would be devalued at a rate of Z$1,000 to Z$1. In other words, what used to cost citizens Z$1 would now require Z$1,000 in currency, and new denominations were printed.

But inflation continued to skyrocket, and the country was forced to revalue the currency again in 2007 and 2008, when the monthly inflation rate reached 231,150,889 percent (that's 231 million percent) in July alone. That same month, the American dollar enjoyed an exchange rate comparable to Z$758,530,000,000. To put all of those zeroes in perspective, in July of 2008, you could take a Z$1 billion bank note out of your wallet and purchase three eggs with it.

In early 2009, the Reserve Bank of Zimbabwe legalized the use of foreign currencies for transactions in their country, and the much-abused Zimbabwean dollar was suspended a few months later "until further notice." It has yet to reappear.

Before all of this economic turmoil, Zimbabwe was a relatively well-developed country for its region. Although the nation suffered through both civil war and political strife in the late 1970s, many citizens had jobs, and some even traveled to America and Europe for vacations. They also attended church. Many Zimbabweans claim to be Christian, and a majority of the population says that they attend religious services regularly, often at mainline denominations, such as Anglican, Methodist, Seventh-day Adventist, and Roman Catholic.

But following the devaluation fiasco, life changed for all but the upper-class minority, including how they arrived at church services. Before the devaluation, most families had a vehicle to use. But afterward, most everyone walked.

Ironically, their sense of community improved as the economy went south. And at one church on the outskirts of Harare, the nation's capital, this made a big difference when a local electrical transformer blew out, cutting off electricity to the entire community.

A local pastor knew that there was little money to replace or repair the generator, so he came up with a unique idea, a version of the old barter system. He walked from house to house, asking families to donate one or two hours of labor to help an engineer from Harare rebuild the machinery and get it back online.

The community benefit was clear, as was the alternative. No work, no electricity.

Within a day or so, with the pastor overseeing the operation, the generator was back in working order, and the community had proved that it could come together to do something for the good of all. The interdependence and trust they had developed in increasingly tough times provided them with a tangible result.

Generosity: "What I Have Is Yours"

When generosity is discussed in the West, the subject almost always centers on money. In America, *generosity* and *money* are virtually interchangeable words. But in the global church, *generosity* means the giving of self—not money, although that can sometimes occur—and any material possession they may have as well. They don't often conceive of giving the way we do, but they clearly have a generous spirit. If you are visiting their home, you have to stay for dinner. It doesn't matter that they don't know where next week's meals are coming from. You're going to share what they have because you're part of the family, part of the community, part of the body of Christ. To them, it as an honor to be generous to a guest, just as it's an honor to be generous to Christ and to His mission.

And that level of generosity captures the full spirit of "what I have is yours."

The apostle Paul tells Timothy to "instruct those who are rich in this present world not to be conceited" (1 Timothy 6:17), so this is clearly a cultural issue of long standing. Then, as now, wealth and possessions cause those who have money and possessions to think that they are—by nature—smarter and better than others. Don't believe it? Fill a room with successful American businessmen and listen in. You'll know right away from their conversation that the vast majority of them believe they have (1) all of the answers, (2) more of what it takes to succeed then the "normal" guys, and (3) deserve everything that they've earned in this life, maybe more.

In the parable of the sower found in Matthew 13, when thorns choke the seeds that fall on the third soil, Jesus describes those thorns as "the worry of the world and the deceitfulness of wealth" (v. 22). The result? The soil becomes unfruitful. Not "less fruitful," but unfruitful, meaning no fruit at all.

So Paul cautions us not to fix our security on riches, "but on God, who richly supplies us with all things to enjoy" (1 Timothy 6:17). This process has everything to do with realizing the resources we have and how to use them wisely, but also to never be defined by them or to allow our security to rest on them. We should always be in a position to pray, "Lord give us this day our daily bread" spiritually, not isolated or insulated by our finances.

The Deceit of Riches and The Dangers of Consumerism

Scripture is very clear that the deceitfulness of riches is a primary cancer in our spiritual lives. But we often don't grasp or see the numbing effect of an abundance of wealth and how it can cause their affections to drift far from the creator of that wealth. Ironically, most of us don't consider ourselves wealthy in any sense of the word. After all, the guy down the street may have "more." But it's all about perspective. It is very easy to maintain that we don't have enough as long as we don't expose ourselves to the material needs of the other 90 percent of the world's population. What is really at work with the deceitfulness of riches is that Satan shifts our frame of reference from the needs of others to a comparative grid of our wants and desires.

Americans are conspicuous consumers, and Satan is the father of consumerism, so it remains one of our primary cultural pressures.

But rather than identify ways to escape from these pressures, we need to recognize and understand them, for when we struggle against them, they will help us align more and more with what God wants us to be. We need to be the church in the midst of a consumer nation, not a church that runs away from it. We are called to be salt and light, not oil and water. The persecuted church doesn't bash their government; they don't bash their neighbors. They take on the pressure of persecution and pain and ask God to use it to align them with His will.

CONSUMERISM IS JUST as dangerous to our souls as . . . persecution is to the souls of those in other countries.

We need to follow their example of how to grow in the midst of a dangerous culture, for consumerism is just as dangerous to our souls as religious or ethnic persecution is to the souls of those in other countries. But they've figured out how to fight against their pressures, and we continue to struggle against ours.

Those pressures we experience take on many different forms, and affect all aspects of the modern Christian life.

For example, in order to attract and evangelize the wealthy, we can fall prey to distorting the gospel to become just another "good thing," another part of life to make it more fulfilling. But if we treat the gospel as an add-on to an already "successful" life—a way to be happier or how to be "better"—we are in real danger of giving people the excuse that once they become followers of Jesus Christ, they need not walk in faith. Instead, this perceived "morality boost" gives some a false feeling of superiority, a "leg-up" to a position of better social standing in the community, which cannot be further from the truth.

When we allow this feeling to remain uncorrected, we sell the gospel short. The contrast in church cultures is very clear, for there is no tangible, earthly benefit to coming to Jesus Christ in the vast majority of the world cultures.

In suburban America, however, there can be a large social benefit. When we accept Christ, we suddenly have a built-in group that's going to be there to help us move, to watch our kids, to help us be a better mom or dad. And we get a whole church directory to network with. We inherit an amazing organizational structure for virtually nothing.

We even hear this subtle belief sometimes in the testimonies shared in church. Instead of, "I was blind and now I see," or "sin had broken me," we hear, "I put this new thing on and it feels good! I love this place!" But we shouldn't be too hard on the new believer, because that message merely echoes one that many churches are promoting: "Come and get your kids plugged in, and you'll get plugged in," and "Look at the happy, healthy faces all around you!" "Come live the blessed life!"

IN THIS CONSUMER MENTALITY . . .

the goal of the gospel shifts subtly from the glory of God to the betterment of "my" life.

In this consumer mentality—which mixes an immense amount of spiritual freedom with large quantities of material-ism—the goal of the gospel shifts subtly from the glory of God to the betterment of "my" life. "Come and get some!" And although that mentality manifests itself in other regions of the world, including parts of Latin American and Africa, it remains strongest in the West. Even in Europe, where the state church dominates, the health and wealth gospel is most pervasive in the pockets of the strongest American influence.

The global church has little or no anticipation of financial blessing or a better station in life; in fact, it's usually the opposite. For example, when believers come to Christ in Japan—a country not normally associated with persecution—families often disown new believers as soon as they are baptized. In Japan, a person will never publicly say they are a Christ-follower until they've been baptized, because that's when they are ostracized. It is a major decision with serious social consequences.

In many instances, we've come to believe that the blessing of faith is a reward of some sort. We may not say it in so many words, but the feeling creeps in that if we read the Bible a lot and pray a lot, when we have to give a presentation in front of our new client, God may give us a little something for our trouble. The blessing comes wrapped in the package we want, and our "obedience" leads to that blessing.

But obedience doesn't lead us to the blessing. Obedience is the blessing.

Pastor and author John Piper got it right when he wrote, "God is most glorified when you are most satisfied in him."[1]

When Is It Easier to Give?

In Luke 21:2–4, Jesus tells the story about the widow and the rich men putting their gifts into the temple treasury: "And He saw a poor widow putting in two small copper coins. And He said, 'Truly I say to you, this poor widow put in more than all of them; for they all out of their surplus put into the offering; but she out of her poverty put in all that she had to live on.' "

This verse implies the question, "When is it easier to be generous?" When you have a lot, or when you have little? The answer to that question will say a lot about how we choose to define generosity.

The Ethiopian church, although resource-poor, has a strong commitment to church planting, and has planted close to a thousand small churches in recent years. In their economy, a church planter can live on $1,200 a year, or $100 a month, so the larger churches in Addis Ababa and other cities ask individuals in their congregations to each give a nickel a month toward missions, and that's where the money comes from. Other churches—some in America—partner with them to provide other necessities such as burros or donkeys, but the monthly support comes largely from the Ethiopian people themselves. A nickel a month is a lot of money for them. But they do it regularly, and gladly.

Giving within a community enhances the lives of all. But something else happens when a church learns to give externally as well.

For years the persecuted church in China has been on the receiving end of aid from the West. Now they are starting to say, "We want to do some of this ourselves." They want the privilege and the opportunity to give, to invest in the lives of others outside of their communities. And following the Sichuan earthquake in 2008, they did a tremendous amount of work toward that goal. House churches mobilized support among the local people in areas hardest hit by the quake, and for the first time in their history, they were a giving church. And they're seeing tremendous benefits out of that. Their community spirit, already at a high level, improved even more. Like the widow bereft of substance, they were willing to give of their talents and substance.

IN ETHIOPIA, it's an honor to support a church planter with a nickel a month.

It's always been a mark of maturity in any church when giving grows beyond the needs of their own local people and their own community to foreign and increasingly distant projects. It's an honor to be generous in God's economy. A church that understands this concept would be honored to be able to share with others what God has shared with them. In Ethiopia, it's an honor to support a church planter with a nickel a month. It's an honor to bring rice for the widows. It's an honor to bring fabric to make things for the orphans.

It's an honor, not an obligation.

Why the Western Church Struggles with Generosity

So why does the Western church struggle with generosity?

In America, our concept of wealth is directly equated to how much money we have. When somebody says, "So-and-so may be poor, but they are rich in relationships" or in some other dimension of life, many in our culture look right past that and think—or even say—"How nice for them. But I need something more tangible."

Yet the often-repeated yet always true testimonial regarding this issue is this: At the end of our days, nobody looks back and says, "I wish I had more money." Instead, we say, "I wish I had more relationships." It has been said and written so many times that it has become a cliché, but that doesn't make it any less true. It is even a hot topic in the secular world in books such as the late Randy Pausch's *New York Times* bestseller *The Last Lecture*, written as death approached the Carnegie Mellon professor of computer science. Nobody seems to disagree with the actual statement, and yet we still chase after money at the expense of relationships.

Why the dichotomy?

There are two ways to view all of the resources on this planet. Simply stated, we can choose to approach life with a mind-set of abundance, which concludes that there is always enough of everything to go around; or with a mind-set of scarcity, which fears that things are going to run out any minute, and—perhaps more importantly—it will probably all be gone before "I get mine."

Guess which category we tend to fall under?

We worry about money in many ways, but one of our primary worries is our fear that we will outlive our money, our ability to earn more, or both. This has already hit home with the generation of men and women who grew up during World War II or the Korean War and began to build their careers during the economic boom of the the 1950s or 1960s. A vast number of them pursued and achieved the "good life." They worked hard, raised families, made solid investments, and became generous givers to their churches and to many other nonprofit organizations.

But because of an extraordinary confluence of recent medical breakthroughs and a really bad economy, their life spans have increased while their pensions and retirement plans have plummeted. Today, many of these generous givers are worried about making ends meet, but are too proud to ask for assistance. They have always had more than enough, and now they are operating out of a scarcity mind-set.

It is very difficult for generosity to exist in the midst of a scarcity mind-set. Like the seed sown on the third soil, weeds eventually choke it off.

For many of us today, still working but wondering about vanishing pension funds and the uncertainty of employment, our giving typically is not sacrificial. Instead, we put twenty, fifty, or even one hundred dollars in the offering and walk out of church feeling like we did something really good. Our guilt may be temporarily assuaged, but our gift did not come from truly caring about others who are poor. Some of us actually "give" solely for tax benefits. In America, statistically speaking, the people who have the most give the least. We're concentrated on our wealth. We're investing it, saving it, and undoubtedly thinking about it when the stock market or 401(k) goes down. When that happens, as it inevitably will, we're the first ones to pull back on giving.

And there's always the problem of debt. Scripture is clear that the debtor is in bondage, and so many of us are locked in metaphorical shackles and chains. It doesn't mean we shouldn't have a mortgage, but that if we have one, we need to have the wherewithal so that mortgage never ties us down.

And as individuals go, so do churches. It's no secret that many American churches of all sizes have big mortgages and big budgets, which at times have made some seek new and better ways to coax money out of their people.

Then you look at the global church. They don't have big edifices to maintain, paint, staff, heat, or cool. Most of the pastors are bi-vocational, so their monetary needs are much smaller.

In Ethiopia and in many other parts of the world, the primary use of their tithes and offerings—after they pay their pastors what they can afford—goes to support church planters and missionaries and the specific needs of those in their communities. It never goes to service debt, for in the persecuted church there is no debt. Giving flows from an understanding of generosity, and from a direct relationship between the giver and the receiver.

The way we use money does not make relationships easier either. On the contrary, our money habits can keep us from developing deeper relationships because they help create a much more formal and official means of exchange. It's always easier to write a check than to serve someone in person. But the way the global church tends to live—often through the exchange of goods and services—generosity not only necessitates, but establishes and deepens, relationship.

There's nothing wrong with money as a means of exchange. It certainly allows us to do things at a distance that we couldn't otherwise accomplish. We can donate, gift, or tithe using credit cards, PayPal, and direct deposit, among many other useful financial services. But each of those methods keeps us from getting person-to-person and eye-to-eye with those in need.

Such practices can have a slow, insulating effect. When all we do is write checks, we move farther from people who are doing good things in other places. Writing checks alone may even keep us from doing the good things God has planned for us.

Yes, a lack of money is one of the great limiters to the overall economic health and prosperity of societies where churches are emerging. Yet who's richer—the person who has all the money in the bank and no friends or connections in the community, or the person with no money and many friends? In America, we often try to figure out how we can still stay financially liquid and comfortable while being sacrificial enough to maintain just enough relationships. Money and its use can often insulate us from people.

WHEN WE GIVE, sometimes there is a feeling that we must be losing something because we have less.

In addition, the motive behind giving can be different in the West. It may be viewed as a way to serve those in desperate need, but there is often an undercurrent of trying to leverage God into getting more back. It's just one more financial transaction.

And it may be more difficult for us to give because giving reveals where our heart is centered. It's hard for us to give because, when we do give, sometimes there is a feeling that we must be losing something because we have less. We depend on our investments and our money; we rely on them to get us through. But the global church is not trying to leverage God for more. They give out of honor and trust and adoration and respect.

And they often give much more than money.

In some regions of the world there simply isn't a lot of money to be had. Few people have a bank account, because there are very few banks. Most people don't even have any pocket change. So it's really true that their wealth is not defined by cash flow. That river is dry.

The global church by and large is a nonmonetary church. When there's something to share it's a physical thing. It's a chicken. It's a bed. And there's something to be said for a community that's constructed out of a barter environment. Where you don't have a neutral exchange like money to give and to buy things, you have to trade what you have for what you need. Sometimes it's simply being who you are, using a God-given skill that puts you in direct personal contact with someone.

The pastor in Latin America who has to paint somebody's house in order for them to give him a chicken so he and his family can eat that week puts himself in a direct relationship with the guy whose house he's painting so that he can minister the gospel.

Paul sat in a marketplace and repaired tents, which enabled him to do a little writing and preaching on the side.

What We Lack

The real richness of global Christians' lives comes not from the amount of money they have in bank accounts—because they don't have them—it's in that intimacy of weaving lives together. In the global church, "not having" is not the same thing as "lacking."

But there is something that we do lack, and it may be the biggest reason why we are not as generous as we could be. More than anything else—more than our debt loads and our formal monetary systems and our attempts to leverage our gifts to God's kingdom for our personal gain—it all comes down to one word: trust.

In the Old Testament, the word *trust* literally meant to fall on your face. Consider this definition in the context of the oft-quoted verse from Proverbs: "Trust in the Lord with all your heart and do not lean on your own understanding. In all your ways acknowledge Him, and He will make your paths straight" (Proverbs 3:5–6).

In other words, "Fall on your face before the Lord, and don't be propped up by what you think you know about anything." But trust is a huge obstacle to many "self-made" Americans, because it is difficult to manifest our own destinies while lying prostrate on the ground before the creator of the universe.

In the global church, trust is simply not an issue. They trust each other so much that they say, "I'm out of food, I need some," or "I'm sick, I need help," or "I'm dying, and I need you to promise me that you'll take care of my kids." It's an authentic, trusting, and interdependent community.

THE GLOBAL CHURCH teaches us is that there should be no shame in being in need.

In contrast, we don't like to owe anyone any favors, or be beholden to our neighbors. For example, when the next-door neighbor and I are mutually dependent—today I'll need him and tomorrow he'll need me—there is no sense of owing. We like that. It's a case of, "I'll scratch his back, and he'll scratch mine." The issue that creates the "I'm beholden to that guy" feeling is rooted in my pride, in the humiliation I feel because I need the help, and the uncomfortable sensation I have that somehow I will have to square it with him before I can feel good again.

Churches sometimes inadvertently help us get around the shame and embarrassment of actually being in need in our culture. Instead of connecting people together in relationship, we have everybody give to a general benevolent fund. If our neighbor loses his job, all he has to do is fill out a private little form, turn it in to the office, and wait until the benevolence committee has a chance to look things over and make a recommendation. It's like the bank loan process, but without putting up any collateral.

And no one has to know anything about his need, especially his friends and neighbors.

But what the global church teaches us is that there should be no shame in being in need. In a society where everybody has nothing and no one has anything, there's absolutely no shame in being in need. The playing field is level. But that's a tough sell in America. How often have we heard several months after the layoff occurred that a good friend lost his job? And even then we probably only heard it because his wife mentioned during her morning Bible study that he wasn't doing well. "What happened?" "Well, he lost his job nine months ago, but he hasn't wanted to tell anybody." That's a very real dynamic in an affluent society. In a money-obsessed culture, when a man loses his job, he loses his identity.

Wouldn't it be better if this sort of giving could happen person to person in small groups or in our neighborhoods? It should be okay to give food to a friend or for them to ask for help. But here's what can happen, and has. Let's say Bob needs $1,000 and Chris has $1,000 to give him. Instead of Chris just handing Bob the money, Chris comes to somebody on the church staff and says, "I want to give Bob a gift of $1,000; how do I get income tax credit for that?" because if Chris gives it to the benevolent fund, which then passes it on to Bob, he gets a tax deduction.

Here again is how something meant for good—something intended to give people the incentive to give to charity—has become a way in which we can try to leverage something done in God's name to get something better for ourselves as well. It isn't wrong to somehow materially benefit from giving, but that possible benefit should never factor into our generosity. Because left to our own calculating hearts, we nearly always tend toward the benefit of the individual (meaning "us") over the benefit of the community.

When we understand the relationship of interdependence and that there is no humiliation in expressing our need to a brother who says, "We're in this together; what I have is yours," and vice versa, it does away with that whole sense of being beholden. For this to work, however, we have to swallow our pride and learn to trust.

But all too often, we are not a trusting people because we have an aversion to being taken advantage of. We don't trust our government leaders; we don't trust our economic institutions; we don't trust our schools or universities; we don't even trust the church to be there for us in hard times.

Occasionally, however, people who have been blessed with financial resources totally get it. They step out in faith and choose to trust the church to help them shed their burden of affluence by teaching them to become generous. Their first step should be to support their local church. It is where their kids and family are taken care of. And it is filled with their neighbors and friends.

But next, they should pick one or two organizations to support financially, chosen not only because of the good stuff they're doing, but also how much they can get personally involved in the doing. In other words, they shouldn't just support an organization that builds quality housing in Mexico; they should travel to Mexico with that organization to help build quality housing. Better still, they should bring their spouse or children or friends along to help as well.

If they travel to Mexico, or anyplace else their generous giving takes them, two things will happen. First, God will use that experience to expand their heart. And second, they'll come home better apprised to how their money's being used. They'll see their money in action, and experience the direct connection with those whom they are serving.

THE BEST GENEROSITY develops out of relationships. That's what we see in the persecuted church.

In the nonprofit world, quality organizations go after people's hearts, not their pocketbooks. They want people to be more deeply involved, because personal involvement brings heart change. Because money is tighter in the current economy, even those with resources are doing their homework before deciding exactly where to be generous. They check on details such as the percentage of giving that actually goes to salary and overhead, and how much goes to the work in the field. Much of this has grown out of the trend toward ministry participation because they feel more strongly about following their money.

But the best generosity is that which develops organically out of relationships. And that's what we see in the persecuted church. That's what we need to learn. It all goes back to our concept of who God is, because when we get that wrong, it leads to all the other mistakes. We don't give generously because we don't understand generosity. We see ourselves as owners, not stewards. And the nonprofit organizations are also at fault, because they may have equated generosity with the size of our gifts and the number of zeroes on our checks instead of the relationships involved.

Being Stewards Serving the Right Boss

Pastors and leaders of nonprofits run organizations that require gifts to survive. They can't barter their way through to the end of the budget year. But at the end of the year, they know that they may end up attracting new donors or givers simply by being good stewards of the resources they have already been given. And good stewardship is vital to a successful nonprofit organization or church.

There is a growing kingdom awareness between many ministries and nonprofit networks that's being driven by donors who are saying, "You need to work together with this other organization that I'm familiar with." It's never a competitive environment when each organization serves the same boss. And that boss is a Jewish carpenter.

Lessons of Trust from the Global Church

So what can we learn from the global church about generosity? We learn that caring is more important than cash flow, that true generosity arises out of shared relationships, and that the full picture is a two-way street. There's one person who wants to care for his neighbor, and there's responsibility on the part of the neighbor to let people know that they have a need.

Again, it all hinges on our ability to trust, or our lack of that ability.

Consider this scenario: While walking down the street in an average American city, we may encounter a woman selling chocolate bars, a man selling oranges, and a couple standing alongside the traffic light, holding a sign that reads "Broke. Hungry. Please Help. God Bless You."

Who is legitimate, and who is not?

We'd probably give money to the lady with the chocolate bars (her kids are obviously involved in some school fund-raiser), we'd be cautious about the man with the oranges (Where were they grown? Were pesticides used?), but we'd probably assume that the couple at the stoplight was just going to go buy themselves some beer.

In America, we do this sort of math in our heads all the time. Unfortunately, some of this way of thinking bleeds over into how we process our giving to the church or donating used items to charity or supporting the work of foreign missions.

In America, it's all about accountability.

But now consider this: Did Jesus ever circle back to check on the people He healed? Did He send back teams to make sure that they were living righteously with their "new" legs and eyes? He healed ten blind men at one time, and yet only one came back to thank Him. Did He send out scouts to track down the other nine to survey them about why they didn't thank Him?

Of course He didn't.

His healing of the blind men—and the lepers, and the paralytic man that was lowered down through the roof, and the woman who grasped His robe in the crowd, and Lazarus—was never merely about those being healed; it was a clear and undeniable demonstration of His power to reverse the effects of sin. He was just setting the table for a larger feast.

In Jesus' own words, "Which is easier, to say to the paralytic, 'Your sins are forgiven'; or to say, 'Get up, and pick up your pallet and walk'?" (Mark 2:9).

In the same spirit, our giving is not about the gift, even though we often try to make it so. The material things that God entrusts to us are not for us. They are for the larger cause, the kingdom work that needs to be accomplished. And whenever we are tempted to acquire money unnecessarily, whenever we begin to hoard, we need to remember the question that Judas asked, in John 12, when Mary took a pound of very expensive ointment and anointed the feet of Jesus.

"'Why was this perfume not sold for three hundred denarii, and given to poor people?' . . . Therefore Jesus said, 'Let her alone, so that she may keep it for the day of My burial. For you always have the poor with you, but you do not always have Me'" (John 12:5, 7–8).

Jesus was very clear to him—and to us—that it's not the monetary value of a gift that is important; it's the quality of devotion that it represents.

Blessed be the God and Father
of our Lord Jesus Christ, who according to His great mercy has caused us
to be born again to a living hope
through the resurrection of Jesus
Christ from the dead, to obtain an
inheritance which is imperishable
and undefiled and will not fade away,
reserved in heaven for you, who are
protected by the power of God
through faith for a salvation ready
to be revealed in the last time.

1 PETER 1:3–5

Therefore I urge you, brethren, by
the mercies of God, to present your
bodies a living and holy sacrifice,
acceptable to God, which is your
spiritual service of worship. And
do not be conformed to this world,
but be transformed by the renewing
of your mind, so that you may prove
what the will of God is, that which
is good and acceptable and perfect.

ROMANS 12:1–2

Epilogue

With the dawn of the second decade of the twenty-first century, the world has turned a good deal of attention to concepts such as environmental sustainability. According to the United States Environmental Protection Agency, "The traditional definition of sustainability calls for policies and strategies that meet society's present needs without compromising the ability of future generations to meet their own needs."[1]

It has been a slow process. In response to the pressure of increasing environmental concerns—which began to gain traction in the 1940s and early 1950s—the 1970 National Environmental Policy Act formally established as a national goal the creation and maintenance of conditions under which humans and nature "can exist in productive harmony, and fulfill the social, economic and other requirements of present and future generations of Americans."

Today, from such diverse disciplines as materials management, public health, and biofuels to climate change, ecosystems, and the study of our man-made environment, research and debate are increasingly focused on the development and creation of "best practices," practices that will do the most good for our fellow human beings while leaving the smallest detrimental impact—often referred to as our "carbon footprint"—on our planet.

Simply put, the concept of sustainable development recognizes that we can't keep doing things the way we always have, that we need to find new approaches to old problems, and that we will need partners to help us find those solutions.

If the twenty-first-century church is to experience an acceptable level of "sustainable development," we must adopt a similar synergistic approach. If we are to fulfill God's desire for His church, we must build on the strengths of the West by learning—and adapting—all we can from our brothers and sisters in the persecuted regions of the world.

Persecution often results in pain, but that same pain can bring perspective, a perspective of who we really are—or can be—in Christ, through God's great mercy.

In the words of the apostle Peter:

> You were not redeemed with perishable things like silver or gold from your futile way of life inherited from your forefathers, but with precious blood, as of a lamb unblemished and spotless, the blood of Christ. For He was foreknown before the foundation of the world, but has appeared in these last times for the sake of you who through Him are believers in God, who raised Him from the dead and gave Him glory, so that your faith and hope are in God. Since you have in obedience to the truth purified your souls for a sincere love of the brethren, fervently love one another from the heart, for you have been born again not of seed which is perishable but imperishable, that is, through the living and enduring word of God. For, "all flesh is like grass, and all its glory like the flower of grass. The grass withers, and the flower falls off, but the word of the Lord endures forever." (1 Peter 1:18–25)

As we have seen throughout this book, the persecuted church is God's gift to us in the West. Their understanding of God, their reverence for His Word, their dependence on prayer and worship, their daily immersion in authentic community, their biblical submission to authority, and their unbridled generosity of spirit can be tremendous resources for us if we only humble ourselves to adopt a spirit of learning.

And when we approach the persecuted church in that spirit of humility, we will experience God's mercy. And thankfully, God's mercies are a renewable resource.

Because of His great faithfulness, they are new every morning.

Notes

Introduction

1. John Canemaker, *Before the Animation Begins* (New York: Hyperion, 1996), 15.
2. Adapted from *A Leader's Guide to After-Action Reviews* (Washington, DC: Department of the Army, 1993), 1–4.

Chapter 1: God and His Word

1. A. W. Tozer, *The Knowledge of the Holy* (New York: Harper & Row, 1961), 6–7.
2. J. I. Packer, *Knowing God* (Downers Grove: InterVarsity Press, 1973), 99.
3. Ibid., 101–102.
4. R. C. Sproul and Robert Wolgemuth, *What's in the Bible* (Nashville: Word/Nelson, 2000), 168.
5. Warren Wiersbe, *The Bible Exposition Commentary: New Testament Volume 1* (Colorado Springs: Cook, 2001), 122.
6. Paul Estabrooks et al., *Standing Strong in the Storm* (Santa Ana, Calif.: Open Doors International, 2003), 216.

Chapter 2: Worship and the Church

1. Paul Estabrooks et al., *Standing Strong in the Storm* (Santa Ana, Calif.: Open Doors International, 2003), 107.
2. Richard Foster, *Freedom of Simplicity* (San Francisco: Harper & Row, 1981), 102–103.

Chapter 3: Prayer and Dependence

1. Paul Estabrooks et al., *Standing Strong in the Storm* (Santa Ana, Calif.: Open Doors International, 2003), 225–226.

Chapter 4: Community, Culture, and Evangelism

1. Reuben Welch, *We Really Do Need Each Other* (Nashville: Impact Books, 1973), 34–35.
2. Dietrich Bonhoeffer, *Life Together* (San Francisco: Harper & Row, 1954), 25–26, 29–30.

Chapter 6: Generosity and Stewardship

   1. John Piper, *The Pleasures of God* (Sisters, Oreg.: Multomah, 2000), 14.

Epilogue

   1. U.S. Environmental Protection Agency, "Sustainability: Basic Information,"
   http://www.epa.gov/sustainability/basicinfo.htm.

Acknowledgments

From Carl Moeller:

My special thanks goes to David Hegg for his willingness to work with me on this project. I knew from the start that Dave and I shared a common heartbeat for Christ and His church. I found out during the project just what an uncommon intellect and servant he is. Thanks, Dave, for giving this book 110 percent of who you are.

Thanks as well to the team at Open Doors USA. I am blessed to serve with some amazing saints—who put their own desires on the back burner in order to serve the persecuted.

From David W. Hegg:

Every worthwhile project is the product of collaboration between committed people. This book perhaps reflects that more than most. My greatest thanks goes to Carl Moeller and the incredible team of faithful Christ-followers at Open Doors USA. Joel Pilcher has been a particularly helpful and enjoyable Open Doors partner in this and many previous projects. Having worked with Open Doors for several years, I continue to marvel at their unwavering faith in Christ, and their radical commitment to champion the cause of those who share our faith but not our freedom.

Thanks as well to Craig Hodgkins for sifting through a mountain of material to find and record our thoughts in one voice. I am also thankful to the dedicated pastors of Addis Ababa who first showed me just how much the American church has to learn.

Finally, thanks goes to my staff team at Grace Baptist Church for their ongoing care to keep my life manageable, and to my incredible wife who keeps our life beautiful and satisfying in the midst of the adventure that is local church ministry. *Soli deo gloria!*

INTO THE MUD

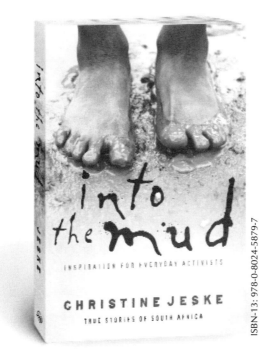

ISBN-13: 978-0-8024-5879-7

Into The Mud takes readers behind the headlines, into real stories of real people living neck-deep in some of Africa's most difficult issues—but with hands, minds, and hearts rooted in God's kingdom. Each of its interwoven stories and related discussion questions addresses a broader issue of missions and development, including: evangelism, literacy and education, microfinance, health services, urbanization and refugee assistance, and more. Reflection questions at the end of each chapter help readers to apply lessons from the chapters to their own ministry contexts.

MOODY
PUBLISHERS

moodypublishers.com

ALWAYS TRUE

Follow bestselling author, speaker, and pastor James MacDonald as he delivers the biblical hope of God's promises in the midst of life's storms. By way of digging into theology, Pastor James uncovers five major categories of promise in the Bible and the five areas about which God repeatedly makes promises. From what to do with fear and doubt to God's goodness, help, and victory—the Bible has much to say about God's presence in our difficulty.

MOODY
PUBLISHERS

moodypublishers.com

World WatchList
Where Faith Costs the Most

WHERE PERSECUTED COUNTRIES ARE RANKED ACCORDING TO THEIR LEVEL OF OPPRESSION

Where are the worst places to live as a Christian? Who are those who lose their jobs, their families and often their lives because they pursue Jesus as Lord and Savior? How can they stand firm in the face of persecution? Each year Open Doors carefully and accurately ranks the worst of the worst and asks you to come alongside your precious brothers and sisters in Christ, come alongside in prayer. Lift them up so they can lift up our God and shine brightly in a cruel and dark world. They request your prayers. Find out more today.

THE WITNESS OF PERSECUTED
CHRISTIANS HAS A UNIQUE
POWER TO REACH A NEW
GENERATION OF LIVES AND
COMMUNITIES THAT WOULD
OTHERWISE NEVER BE OPEN
TO THE GOSPEL—
BUT THEY CANNOT DO IT ALONE.

Open Doors®
Serving persecuted **Christians** worldwide
www.OpenDoorsUSA.org/WorldWatchList

For those outside the USA go to: **www.OpenDoors.org** to find an office near you.